Spirits of Dallas
The Haunting of the Big D

Brian Righi

Schiffer Publishing Ltd

4880 Lower Valley Road, Atglen, Pennsylvania 19310

Copyright © 2008 by Brian Righi
Library of Congress Control Number:
2008930571

Designed by
Stephanie Daugherty
Type set in CastleT/
NewBskvll BT

ISBN:
978-0-7643-3036-0

Printed
in China

Schiffer Books are available at special discounts for bulk purchases for sales promotions or premiums. Special editions, including personalized covers, corporate imprints, and excerpts can be created in large quantities for special needs. For more information contact the publisher:

Schiffer Publishing Ltd.
4880 Lower Valley Road
Atglen, PA 19310
Phone: (610) 593-1777
Fax: (610) 593-2002
E-mail: Info@schifferbooks.com

Please visit our web site catalog at
www.schifferbooks.com

We are always looking for people to write books on new and related subjects. If you have an idea for a book, please contact us at the above address.

This book may be purchased from the publisher. Include $5.00 for shipping. Please try your bookstore first. You may write for a free catalog.

In Europe, Schiffer books are distributed by:
Bushwood Books
6 Marksbury Ave.
Kew Gardens
Surrey TW9 4JF
England
Phone: 44 (0)208 392-8585
Fax: 44 (0)208 392-9876
E-mail: Info@bushwoodbooks.co.uk
Website: **www.bushwoodbooks.co.uk**
Free postage in the UK. Europe: air mail at cost.

Dedication
For my brother
Joseph Righi,
a natural-born
ghost hunter

Acknowledgements

By the time a work such as this travels from my computer screen and into your hands it has relied on countless individuals to give it birth. Writing isn't really some solitary, magical process, despite the way we writers brag, but a matter of many people working very hard for never enough pay.

Having cleared the air of this dreadful misconception, I want to take a moment before we start our tale and thank a few of the people that made this possible. So please put your hands together for Dinah Roseberry and the folks at Schiffer Publishing, for all their hard work and dedication to producing quality books; for Angela Conley and her knowledge of photography (but most importantly for her love); and for my ghost hunting pals at DFW Ghost Hunters, for joining me on many of my adventures.

In addition, I want to thank all the other paranormal investigators who shared their time, expertise, and passion for ghost hunting with me. Also let us not forget the citizens of Dallas, both past and present, who gave us all one amazing city. Finally, I want to thank you the reader for your love of ghost stories.

Contents

Back in the Saddle Again

When I first began investigation the supernatural world of ghosts for a book entitled *The Ghosts of Fort Worth: Investigating Cowtown's Most Haunted Locations*, I have to admit that I didn't have a clue as to what I was getting myself into. Stumbling through creepy cemeteries at night looking for ghosts to interview may seem like pure folly to some, but through trial and error, it provided a wealth of experience. After countless investigations, interviews, and hours spent rifling through dusty library shelves, my filing system was bulging with reports of hauntings from all over Texas. From tales of phantom hitchhikers still thumbing rides to reports of spectral cowboys driving ghostly herds across the moonlit prairie, it was all there waiting to be told.

When the book was finished, my intentions were to move on to more pedestrian topics and leave all this "ghost nonsense" behind. Yet each time I set my pen to paper, all I could think about was that stack of files in the corner threatening to topple over. There were still too many unanswered questions remaining and more than a few adventures left to be had. I knew then and there it was no use fighting the urge, and so turned my attention to the ghostly legends of Dallas, Texas.

It became clear that Dallas would be a city unlike any that I had seen before; a city built on big ideas and even bigger dreams. Perhaps that's why so many of the wonderful people who live there have come to refer to it in that distinctive Lonestar twang of theirs as the "Big D."

John Neely Bryan

In fact, you could say it was one of those big ideas that started it all when John Neely Bryan came to

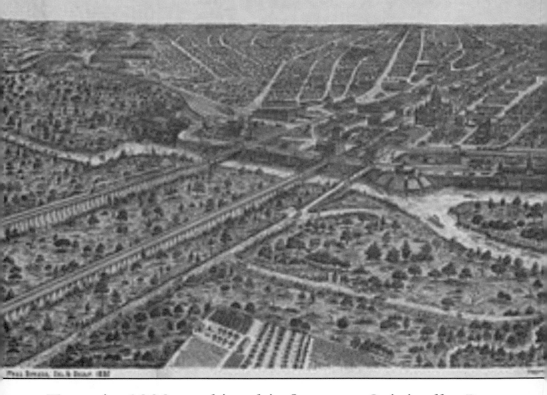

Dallas, Texas. Geography and Map Division, Library of Congress, Paul Giraud 1892.

Texas in 1839, seeking his fortune. Originally, Bryan hoped to establish a lucrative trading post that would serve both the native Indians and the westward moving wagon trains of settlers looking for a new home. The natural choice for just such a venture turned out to be a stretch of land resting on the eastern banks of the Trinity River where shallow fords allowed easy crossing along routes used by both Indians and settlers alike.

Unfortunately, Bryan's dream of a commercial empire evaporated before it even began. Upon returning home to Arkansas to prepare for the endeavor, a treaty was signed removing all of the native tribes from the area. For Bryan, that amounted to about half of his expected business and, for a lesser man, that might have ended it all right there. Instead, he simply came up with an even bigger idea.

In 1841, Bryan built a small log cabin on the bluffs overlooking the Trinity River and proclaimed it the new settlement of Dallas. To this day, the origin of the name is still something of a controversy for historians. Some claim that it was named after the local politician George Mifflin Dallas, but others contest that George Dallas did not become popular until after the founding of the city. Bryan would be of little help in the debate either; simply stating that he named it after a close friend. Regardless of whose name it came to bare, soon after it was established, the tiny hamlet began to grow under the driving force of Bryan. Not only was he responsible for the founding of the settlement, but also went on to become its postman, grocer, and for a time his cabin became the courthouse.

When gold was discovered at Sutter's Mill, California, in January of 1848, the resulting gold rush that followed sparked a massive movement westward. Over 300, 000 would-be prospectors arrived from corners of the world as far away as Asia, Europe, and South America. Many passed through the small town of Dallas on their way to the cold mountain streams of California in pursuit of their dreams of wealth. Not only did this swell the population of Dallas, but more than a few of its citizens got caught up in the gold craze themselves. Even the industrious Bryan ran off with a pick and a pan to seek his fortune, and like most, he returned a short time later with little more than he started with.

A Growing Dot on the Map

Despite a steady influx of immigrants including French, Belgian, Swiss, German, and African Americans, Dallas continued to remain a tiny dot on the map. It wasn't until after the American Civil War, when the first passenger trains started arriving that the city developed into a major shipping center for the southwest. The story goes that just prior to this, in a desperate bid to attract the Houston and

Central Texas Railroad, the city offered them a bribe of $5,000 to move their tracks twenty miles south to Dallas. When the rail lines were completed however, the city found that it could not actually come up with the promised money. Instead, they sneaked a bill through legislation forcing the railroad to honor the move anyway.

With its newfound growth and prosperity came another consequence—the outlaws. Desperados and gunslingers filled the taverns, gambling parlors, and dance halls that seemed to spring up over night. Colorful characters such as Belle Starr, who began her career as a dance-hall girl before turning horse thief, and Sam Bass, who robbed four trains in two months, made their mark here. Even the famous Doc Holiday opened a dentist's shop in town before riding off into the history books at the O.K. Corral.

None-the-less, it was progress that eventually tamed the wild streets of Dallas more than the hangman's noose or the lawman's gun. With the advent of the city's industrial period, the free spirited gunmen that once roamed its thoroughfares melted back into the dime-store novels they seem to have come from.

In time, Dallas moved from a center for ranching and farming to a fully self-sustaining metropolitan area. Even the great depression, which swept across America in the 1930s, could not diminish its spirit. Despite the harsh economic climate of the times, the city flourished even more, due in large part to the discovery of something they called "black gold" or "Texas tea."

In 1930, one year after the infamous stock market crash, seventy-year-old wildcatter Columbus Marion Joiner struck oil on a farm one hundred miles east of Dallas. The Texas oil boom that followed assured the city's financial success and positioned it to become a center for the oil industry in Texas and Oklahoma. Even today the oil industry in an integral part of the economy of the city as well as north Texas and the sight of oil wells are still a common feature of the landscape.

Since the time that John Bryan first founded the tiny settlement over 150 years ago, Dallas has grown from a few scattered cabins along the banks of a river to a sprawling metropolis of over one million people. Yet against the hustle and bustle of the big city that it became, Dallas has maintained a rich tradition of storytelling culled from the diverse ethnic, cultural, and religious roots of its early citizens. The African Americans, Hispanics, Asians, and Europeans that came to this city packed more than just beans and bullets into their wagons. They also brought with them the tales and superstitions of their native lands, which they blended into the scenery of their new home. This in turn gave rise to a city deliciously haunted by the dark tales of ghosts. From street corners to store fronts, bars to barbershops, everywhere I went someone knew of a place that they claimed to be haunted.

A Two-Pronged Approach

After a while, trying to investigate them all quickly turned into a daunting task; therefore I decided on a two-pronged approach when determining which leads to follow. The first was to include those places that could be accessed by the reader in the hopes that they too would have the opportunity to visit the sites and scare up a few ghosts of their own. The second was to consider places that painted a picture of the city itself. I wanted the reader to understand all of the history and human drama that made the city of Dallas what it is today. In short, I wanted them to love the story as much as did.

With that in mind, please join me if you will on an amazing journey through the supernatural world of ghosts as we investigate the spirits of the "Big D."

And the Band Played On

The Adolphus Hotel.

At the Adolphus there's a ballroom
On the 19th floor, upstairs
Its phantoms trace the dances
Of Ginger Rogers and Fred Astaire

—David Davis,
Director of Public Relations
for the Adolphus Hotel

For the first act, I decided to jump in with both feet and investigate a lead that would take me to the bustling heart of the city itself, where phantom guests were said to haunt the decades old Adolphus Hotel. Known as the grand dame of the Dallas hotel set, the towering edifice has come to represent all the wealth, flamboyance, and prestige the city has to offer—a place that over the years has attracted the likes of movie stars, politicians, and European royalty, including George W. Bush and Queen Elizabeth II.

Located in the upscale Main Street District of downtown Dallas, the twenty-one story Texas landmark has even been referred to by its critics as "the most beautiful building west of Venice." For me, spending the night hunting ghosts amid the splendor of such an opulent place promised a wonderful departure from the damp cemeteries and drafty buildings I was used to.

Unlike many that come to the hotel in search of a good night's rest, my suitcase would not contain the usual traveler's fare. Instead of shampoo and tube socks, mine would carry an assortment of ghost hunting gadgets essential to any good investigation. You name it, motion detectors, night vision cameras, and electromagnetic field meters (EMFs), it all went into the bag. For hygiene sake, I did remember to pack a toothbrush however; nothing chases the living or the dead away faster than bad breath.

The Beer Baron and His Castle

In 1910, the Missouri beer baron, Adolphus Busch of the Anheuser-Busch Brewing Association was approached by city leaders with the proposition of building a luxury hotel that would meet the needs of the growing metropolis. In short order, a deal was hashed out carrying with it two important stipulations. The first was that city leaders had to invest in the project as well, and the second was that Adolphus could build it on any spot he wanted to.

Dallas readily agreed to the proposal and the project was soon underway. Adolphus wanted his hotel to be the best and that meant it needed the best location, which happened to be already occupied by Dallas's city hall at the time. Nevertheless, city officials promptly tore down the 1889 municipal building and turned the property over for construction.

After two years of frantic activity, the Adolphus Hotel opened its doors to the first guests on October 5, 1912. Built by architects Barnett, Hayes, and Barnett of St. Louis, the hotel embodied many of the major elements found in the French Renaissance Beaux-Arts style. The 1.87 million dollar, red-brick building was a profusion of balustrades, bas—relief panels, and sculptured figures crowned with a slate and bronze roof. Topping it all off, (fitting for a beer baron) was a turret in the corner of the building suggestively shaped like a German beer stein.

Many would also later suggest that Adolphus Busch's sense of the symbolic didn't stop there, and that the number of floors was meant to correspond to the fact that Adolphus Busch was the twenty-first of twenty-two children. With so many floors, the Adolphus Hotel soared to an amazing height of 312 feet, making it the tallest building in Texas at the time. It would continue to hold the record until being eclipsed by the Magnolia Petroleum Building just down the street in 1922.

Unfortunately, Adolphus Busch died in a Bavarian Castle on October 10, 1913, without ever having spent a night in his magnificent hotel. Over the years, the hotel underwent a series of expansions in an effort to keep pace with the city sprouting up around it.

In 1916, a U-shaped fourteen-story addition was constructed to the west of the hotel, followed by another twenty-three-story addition in 1926. When it was all said and done, a final twenty-two-story complex went up to the rear of it placing the total number of rooms at the time to around twelve hundred. As a result of its long and outstanding history, the Adolphus Hotel was added to the National Register of Historic Places in 1983.

If These Walls Could Talk

Arriving in front of the immense structure shortly before nightfall, it was a bit humorous to watch the curious expression on the face of the doorman as he lifted my bulky bags of equipment onto the hotel luggage dolly. The Adolphus Hotel might have played host to kings and movie stars, but I doubt its seen many ghost hunters. Once inside however, I was astounded by the opulence of the place, with interior spaces detailed in lavish wood trim, vaulted ceilings covered in murals by Alexander Rosenfeld, and hand-blown crystal chandeliers of seventeenth-century design. It was enough to take my breath away.

Following the doorman down hallways, past identical rows of white doors on the 19th floor, I could not help but imagine all of the history that had occurred here. It's the type of place that brings to mind such cliques as "if these walls could talk, imagine all the stories they would tell." Yet unknown to most, behind its normal hotel façade, there were secrets lurking about, questions within the very walls themselves, and beneath it all, there were ghosts waiting.

Over the years, guests occupying the 19th floor have reported a number of unexplained events that point to ghostly activity. Some have heard the muffled drone of piano music coming through their walls; only when they called the front desk to complain, they were told the room adjacent to theirs was empty. Others recount hearing the sounds of big band music blaring through the halls at night accompanied by the noise of partygoers stomping and dancing. Yet when hotel security is dispatched to the scene, all they find are empty hallways softly carpeted and quiet.

However, a close look at the history of the 19th floor might be a key in shedding some light on the noisy mystery. Interestingly enough, it was this floor that once held the building's grand ballroom before renovations gutted it to make

Corridor where the phantom sounds of partygoers still linger.

way for additional guest suites. The 1930s, were a different matter, though, and the ballroom was the hot spot where Dallas's elite danced the night away to the sounds of Jimmy Dorsey, Benny Goodman, and Glen Miller. The subsequent remolding of the 1970s, sealed off the old ballroom, resigning it to a dark cavity at the heart of the colossal hotel.

Now according to John Valis, hotel Director of Engineering, there's only one way to reach the lost ballroom. On the 21st floor, behind an undisclosed door, there's a hidden crawlspace, which leads to a catwalk spanning the ceiling of the 19th floor. Below this is the lost ballroom of the Adolphus Hotel. Of course it's not what it used to be; insulation now covers the hard-wood floors where dancers once jitterbugged and strips of wallpaper hang from the walls behind the bandstand. Now it's merely a place forgotten by most, forgotten even by time itself, but perhaps not by the spirits of those who spent so many happy evenings here.

Phantoms of the Past

There is one theory common among researchers of the paranormal that may help explain this unusual activity known as a residual haunting. Over time, the environment of a location absorbs the energy within it. The stronger the energy produced, such as emotions of love or hate, the more powerful a receptor the place becomes. The wood, walls, furniture, etc., all become highly charged objects that release the energy again when the appropriate trigger is found. This can amount to anything from certain weather conditions to someone entering the area that is sensitive enough to receive the energy. The released energy then creates a scene or reenactment that projects itself like a movie on the big screen. For instance, think of how a phonograph works. Groves are etched in the record's surface that when struck by the phonograph's needle produce music, or in this case, ghostly melodies from a band that played long ago.

Back in my room, I began fine tuning my audio equipment and checking the walls with a physician's stethoscope for odd sounds. With enough wires snaking about the room to trip over, I grabbed my trusty camera and was off wandering the halls in search of noisy ghosts. The phantom music was just the tip of the iceberg I would learn, and the guests weren't the only ones encountering things they could not explain. Even the well-mannered and meticulous staff here has reported strange feelings of being watched by an unseen presence while going about their duties. Dale Rust, the hotel bartender, will tell you over a good stiff drink that a playful spirit loves to rearrange the bottles behind the bar. Any attempt to place them in their proper order only leads to them being moved again when his back is turned.

Other employees are fond of recounting, in rather hushed tones, the story of a customer who frequented the hotel for years. For weeks after her death, her image appeared repeatedly at her favorite table in the bistro's seating area.

In another case of ghostly sightings, two women are said to have fled the hotel in a panic late one night after waking to find the apparition of a man standing in their bedroom.

The most common tales, told by guests and staff alike, involve the legend of a jilted bride. It's said that in the 1930s, a young bride-to-be was left standing at the altar in the ballroom on the 19th floor. Overwhelmed by the shame and grief of the slight, she returned to her empty honeymoon suit and hung herself. Since that time, the sounds of a crying woman have been heard coming from rooms that are unoccupied. Others have felt her presence in the form of a hot wind rushing through the corridors, leaving those in its path with an immense feeling of sadness. In one incident, the windows of a suite burst open from a violent force of air causing several of the room's guests to fall over themselves in their rush to escape.

After discretely snapping as many photos as I thought hotel security would let me get away with, I returned to my room to call it a night. I was hoping that my noisy spirit neighbors would be rude enough to keep me up all night with their loud music and rambunctious partying.

Truth be told, I slept like a baby in one of the biggest, softest beds I have ever laid down in. Whether or not you believe that ghostly partygoers relive the good times from dusk till dawn or that the tragic phantom of a doomed bride stalks the halls, the Adolphus hotel will not give up her secrets easily. The next morning, as the doorman hailed a taxi for me, I could only sigh and think that ghost hunting can be such hard work at times.

The Adolphus Hotel
1321 Commerce Street
Dallas, Texas 75202
Phone: 214.742.8200
Web: www.hoteladolphus.com

Portrait of a Ghost

Majestic Theatre.

The mundane creates its own horror
through the memories forced on it by former owners.

—Stacy Graham

There's an old saying that "a picture is worth a thousand words," but at the Majestic Theatre, on the eastern edge of Dallas's downtown district, there's a painting that just may hold a great deal more. Some have even come to suspect that it possesses the discarnate spirit of the theatre's former owner who rises each night to haunt the building.

Located on Elm Street, the historic structure rises above the jostling city streets, congested with the sounds of traffic horns and neverending construction. It almost seems out of place against the towering urban landscape that surrounds it. Yet what it lacks in shear size is certainly made up for in the influence it's had on the city's history. I wasn't here to catch a show, however; I was here to catch a ghost.

Lights, Camera, Action

In the 1920s, a jack of all trades named Karl Hoblitzelle rolled into town seeking to make his fortune. Hailing from St. Louis, Missouri, as one in a line of thirteen siblings, Karl had tried his hand at just about everything from real estate to soap making. With little more than a few years of elementary school under his belt, Karl moved from one job to another until one day he discovered the stage. Not that he could sing or dance mind you, but he was a showman and more importantly, knew what audiences wanted.

Ever the innovator, he realized the potential vaudeville acts held if they could be censored enough to appeal to the average American family. Vaudeville had always carried a seedy reputation wherever it went with high-kicking burlesque dancers, flashy musicians, and racy comics. To pull it off, Karl would need to do more than just take the show out of the saloon; he would have to take the saloon out of the show. To achieve the dream, Karl and his brothers pooled their resources together, attracted investors, and formed the Interstate Amusement Company.

The plan was simple, build a series of theatres throughout the southwest and stock them with the best family-friendly vaudeville acts money could buy. Soon vaudeville houses were springing up in Fort Worth, Waco, and San Antonio, but the company's flagship and showcase piece would come to be the Majestic Theatre in Dallas.

Built at a cost of two million dollars by famed Chicago architect John Eberson in 1921, the five-story building followed a Renaissance Revival design popular at the time. Tripartite windows set in arched frames spread across the front, along with elaborate moldings, and an ornamental cornice to crown the work. The interior was an integration of various styles, which later became known as "atmospheric." Everything about the place, from the front doors to the fixtures, was created to wow theatergoers with an illusion that transported them to another time and place. Decorative Corinthian columns shouldered massive ceilings while murals portraying ancient pastoral themes filled the walls. Upon entering the lobby, marble floors sparkled in well-polished brilliance as huge twin staircases rose to the auditorium's entrances. Envisioned with a "Roman gardens" theme in mind, the theatre even included a marble fountain copied from an original piece in the Vatican gardens of Rome.

Despite the grandiosity that awaited the average visitor when they first entered, the crème de la crème of the theatre experience was still the fan-shaped 2,400-seat auditorium. Here one could sit back and gaze on a ceiling painted to look like floating clouds with mechanically controlled twinkling lights. All these, remember, were before the modern age of expensive special effects. Other innovations, although less glamorous, were no less important to Karl's philosophy of catering to the American family. The theatre boasted its very own nursery for patrons with small children called Majestic Land, complete with a petting zoo and indoor carousel.

When the grand opening of the Majestic Theatre occurred on April 11, 1921, it was nothing short of spectacular. Spotlights, limousines, and celebrities turned up for a performance by famed vaudeville actress Olga Petrova, in a scene to rival any modern red-carpet Hollywood premiere.

Even with all the razzle-dazzle of vaudeville, its time would come and go as the era of talking pictures emerged with the showing of *The Jazz Singer* in October of 1927. Keeping up with the times was an easy thing for a man like Karl Hoblitzelle, who made sure to keep his finger on the pulse of what the American public wanted.

Soon, the Majestic was hosting movie premieres for stars as big as Jimmy Stewart, Gregory Peck, and John Wayne. The fun didn't stop there, however, and the Majestic continued its tradition of live entertainment with performances by some of the hippest big bands in the country. Legendary greats such as Duke Ellington and Cab Calloway filled the air with their musical genius as Dallasites Lindy Hopped the night away to swooning saxophones and dancing piano cords. By the 1960s, the theatre was at its peak with lines for movie tickets and other shows stretching completely around the block.

In 1967, Dallas's greatest showman, Karl Hoblitzelle died in his home and was returned to his native city of St. Louis for burial. He was a man that had risen from the ranks of common men to become a driving force for the entertainment industry of an entire city. More than that, he was an innovator with a flare for the dramatic and a deep love for the American family.

His beloved Majestic would struggle on for only a short time after his death. New theatres were springing up every day in the increasingly expanding suburbs that surrounded Dallas. That meant moviegoers didn't have to drive all the way into the city to enjoy their favorite blockbusters. Now there were shinny new mega theatres just down the street. The Majestic finally "went dark" on July 16, 1973, after the last showing of the smash hit James Bond film *Live and Let Die*.

For almost three years, the landmark theatre moldered away, becoming nothing more than an expensive home for mice and pigeons. Then on January 31, 1976, the Hoblitzelle Foundation, which still owned the building, donated it to the city of Dallas.

Realizing its worth, restorations were quickly undertaken to renovate the Renaissance exterior of the building to its former glory. The interior got quite the touch up as well and improvements in acoustics, seating, lighting, and stage renovation fully modernized the theatre without compromising its original feel. When the now 1,704-seat Majestic Theatre reopened on January 28, 1983, it was named to the National Register of Historic Places. Today, it continues to serve the city of Dallas proudly as a venue for Broadway plays and musicals.

A Spirited Showing

The Majestic has been home to many talents in the eighty-six years that it's been in business. Everyone from comedians to musicians, and movie stars to magicians have graced its stage, but now some believe that the theatre is also playing host to a spirit as well.

Ronnie Jessie, the former Program Director for the Majestic, reports he's had a few encounters with the resident spirit himself. Some evenings when he was alone, the telephone lines would light up as if in use by someone in the building.

Most telling however, is a story related to him by one of the security guards working the late shift. One evening, while making his rounds, the guard passed through the darkened auditorium when a backdrop suspended above the stage began descending slowly as if on cue. Thinking someone was behind the stage's curtain, he called out the names of several people that might still be working. No one answered. Exploring the auditorium and stage carefully, he could find no one present. The odd fact he noted was that in order to drop the scenery, a crank needed to be turned manually by hand. If it was a case of the mechanism slipping, then the backdrop would have spilled onto the stage and quickly unrolled.

Another former member of the Majestic staff, Managing Director Celia Barshop, also reports having a brush with the ghost. Walking through the building early one Saturday morning, she suddenly smelled the strong aroma of food cooking. She first checked the commercial kitchen on the second floor, but it was empty and there were no signs of recent cooking. She then headed to her office to turn on the lights, but she still couldn't shake the smell of food. In the main lobby, the smell was even stronger and she couldn't help but feel overwhelmed by the sensation that someone else was in the building with her. Heading back to the kitchen, she pushed the swinging door open and jammed a wooden stopper under it. After scouring the trashcans, pots, and refrigerators looking for some clue to the smell, she checked the stovetops; they were cold. When she turned to leave the kitchen, the door was closed. Spooked by the experience she called out as bravely as she could to the would-be ghost that "if it didn't hurt her, she certainly wouldn't bother it."

Others have experienced a gamut of paranormal activity in the theatre including cold spots, sensations of being touched, and disembodied voices. None of which, the Office of Cultural Affairs for the Majestic reports ever appears harmful or threatening. In fact, they claim they rather like having the ghost around the office, kind of livens things up a bit.

Many eyewitnesses to these and other strange events have come to the conclusion that the benign spirit haunting the theatre is none other than Karl Hoblitzelle himself. Some reason that he has returned from the grave to make sure his beloved theatre is being run properly, while others think that old Karl just loved the stage so much that even in death he couldn't give up the spotlight.

Most agree, however, that a portrait of Karl Hoblitzelle, once located in the 5th floor conference room of the theatre may be the source of the haunting. Those who have gazed upon the white-jacketed figure of the old man in the portrait often walk away with an unsettling feeling. Almost as if the painting had a life of its own, the cold stare of the figure within it seems to follow them about the room, watching their every move. It's a feeling most cannot shake when they first encounter the portrait, which has led to the belief that the spirit of Karl Hoblitzelle resides in the painting itself.

The Majestic's auditorium and scene of paranormal activity.

Courtesy of the Majestic Theatre.

Karl Hoblitzelle Has Left the Building

Walking through the theatre alone, I listened to my feet echo against the marble floor while snapping away with my camera in the hopes of picking up some proof of paranormal activity. The current manager, John Wilborn, was kind enough to answer my questions about the place, but was keen to point out that since his tenure at the Majestic, nothing out of the ordinary has occurred.

That is perhaps because, for some reason, the portrait was moved to an undisclosed location, which corresponds roughly to the time when the haunting ceased. Try as I might, I couldn't get anyone at the theatre to tell me where the painting was shipped off to or even why it was removed to begin with. Granted, I was disappointed in not being able to meet Karl Hoblitzelle face to face, but I did get a wonderful tour of this beautiful theatre.

It's true that ghosts have been known to haunt objects as well as locations or people. The history of paranormal research is replete with examples of everything from jewelry to furniture carrying along a few ghosts with them. Normally, the objects in question were known to the deceased during their lifetime and had some sentimental value or meaning to them. After death, they find their spirit drawn back to the object, unable to let go and move on to the next world. In most cases, once the object in question was removed from the scene, the haunting stopped altogether. Could the spirit of Karl Hoblitzelle be attached to the portrait of himself or are there other answers?

James Todd, professor of psychology at Ohio State University, co-authored a study on the visual effects that pictures have on observers. What he found is that if a person in a painting or photograph looks straight ahead, the observer's perception will do the rest. Regardless of the angle or vantage, the figure's eyes in the painting will appear the same; it's the observer who compensates for the change, giving the illusion that the eyes of that painting are following them wherever they go.

Optical illusion or not, somewhere, perhaps in some dark storage closet sits the forgotten painting of a man long deceased whose spirit waits for the chance to rise again.

The Majestic Theatre
1925 Elm Street
Dallas, Texas 75201
Phone: 214.880.0137
Web: www.dallassumermusicals.org

Shadows of the Past

Sixth Floor Museum.

History is the memory of a nation.

—John F. Kennedy

On November 22, 1963, a procession of dark limousines made their way slowly into the large basin-like square of Dealey Plaza surrounded by heavy police escort and the ever-present secret service. It was an uncharacteristically warm day for late November, as over 200,000 of Dallas's citizens lined the parade route to pay tribute to President John F. Kennedy as he entered the city. Riding in an open-topped limousine with his wife, Jacqueline, and Texas Governor John Connally and his wife, Nellie, President Kennedy waved to the cheering crowds. Watching the spectators filling the streets, the governor's wife turned to the smiling President and uttered the last words he would ever hear, "Mr. President, you cannot say Dallas doesn't love you."

A Tragedy Unfolds

At approximately thirty minutes past noon, the motorcade turned sluggishly onto Elm Street and was advancing on the Texas School Book Depository when the first of the shots rang out. Bystanders in the crowd dived for cover and watched helplessly as the President's body jerked violently and then slumped over in his seat. The first round to strike the president entered his upper back and penetrated the neck before exiting his throat. The second shot sounded just as a large hole exploded from the right side of the President's head, covering the car's interior and nearby motorcycle officer with blood and brain tissue. Governor Connally was struck as well, with a bullet ripping through his back, chest, right wrist, and left thigh. The limousine sped away in a sudden rush of police sirens, but it proved too late, and at 1 PM, the thirty-fifth president of the United States was pronounced dead at Parkland Memorial Hospital.

Bob Jackson, a *Dallas Times Herald* reporter accompanying the presidential motorcade later recalled that in the chaos of the shooting, he noticed the muzzle of a rifle jutting from a corner window on the sixth floor of the book depository.

That day, a nation stood stunned by the murder of its beloved president. In the first hours of the assassination, the country reeled in confusion. Adults wept openly and gathered in one another's living rooms to watch the coverage on television. Traffic in some areas came to a halt as radio announcers decried the news and schools across the nation closed early.

The Texas School Book Depository would later be identified as the sniper's nest from which the assassination was carried out after spent shell casings and an Italian

Mannlicher-Carcano bolt-action rifle were discovered on the sixth floor. Forensic science wasn't what it is today, but that evidence coupled with finger and palm prints linked an order clerk named Lee Harvey Oswald to the shooting.

Oswald, an ex-marine and known communist sympathizer, was seen on the sixth floor that day just thirty-five minutes before the motorcade passed. In addition, other witnesses reported him leaving the building in a hurry a mere two minutes after the shooting. He was later arrested for both the Kennedy assassination and the murder of a Dallas patrolman in the Oak Cliff section of the city.

The Texas School Book Depository

Even today, almost fifty years later, the Texas School Book Depository stands as a tragic reminder of the events that occurred there, but what many fail to realize is that the history of the site extends well beyond that. Included as part of John Neeley Bryan's 1841 land claim, it first passed into the hands of George and Mary Braird, who built a house and slave quarters on the property. When the family grew too large for the home they packed up and moved on, but the main structure remained in use as a boarding house for a number of years.

By 1882, the area began changing and most of the original structures on the block were razed to make room for the coming railroad and the city's new industrialized zone. In 1894, Phil L. Mitchell, President and Director of the Rock Island Plow Company, a farm equipment company headquartered in Rock Island, Illinois, purchased the property for $9,000. In four years time, the company erected a five-story structure to house its offices and showrooms, but fate would have its own way. Shortly after construction, lightening struck the building setting it ablaze. Undeterred, the company rebuilt the structure as it stands today, adding an additional two floors to the previous design.

The building continued to house various commercial enterprises until the Texas School Book Depository moved in around 1963. As a privately owned company charged with filling the book orders of public schools across the southwest, the first four floors of the building were devoted to book sellers, while the remaining floors were utilized as storage.

After the tragic events on November 22, 1963, the school book depository continued to operate out of the location until moving in 1970. The current owner, an oil tycoon named Colonel D. Harold Byrd, then sold the property at auction to Aubrey Mayhew, a Nashville music promoter and Kennedy memorabilia collector. Mayhew planned to establish a Kennedy museum on the sixth floor, but when the financing fell through, he defaulted on the $650,000 in loans and the building went to foreclosure.

Following an arsonist's attempt to burn it down, Colonel Byrd repurchased the property, and in doing so, saved the landmark from the city's wrecking ball. Dallas County then purchased the property in 1977, and renamed it the Dallas County Administration Building, which today houses the seat of the Dallas County Government.

Quick to capitalize on the building's unique place in history, the city then stepped forward and raised almost 3.5 million dollars, and on Presidents' Day, February 20, 1989, opened a museum on the sixth floor. Operated by the nonprofit Dallas County Historical Foundation, an estimated half million people pass through the 9,000-square-foot museum each year. With tastefully interpretive exhibits of artifacts, photographs, and video presentations, the museum examines the life, death, and legacy of President John F. Kennedy in the context of American history. Even the shooter's nest in the southeast corner of the building is preserved much as it was the day of the assassination; sealed off from time and the elements behind thick glass.

The museum may have preserved much of its earlier look and feel for the sake of posterity, but the industrial zone that once sprang up around it changed considerably with building booms in the 1970s, and 1980s. Now, thanks to the preservation efforts of groups like the one responsible for the rebirth of the Sixth Floor Museum, the west end of Dallas's downtown has become a historic district. Many of the late nineteenth-century warehouses that once helped fuel the city's commercial endeavors now play host to trendy restaurants and shops designed to attract tourists.

The Spirit of the Sixth Floor

Yet the story of that terrible day doesn't end there, and some claim that the museum holds more than just dusty bits and pieces of the past. Since the museum's opening, the sixth floor has been plagued by the presence of a dark spectral being, often seen stalking through its exhibit-filled chambers.

The unusual shadow-like figure can normally be glimpsed only out of the corner of the eye or just as it's rounding a corner. Those foolish enough to follow the ghost, or get a better look, usually find it disappearing right before they can catch up to it. In a number of these cases severe cold spots followed in its ghostly wake, with many of the sightings occurring near the southeast corner where the sniper's nest is located.

A number of visitors to the sniper's nest exhibit further report strange sensations of regret and sadness overwhelming them. Most describe the feeling as something distinctively alien, as if a dark cloud or presence hovered about the scene forcing itself upon them.

Photographic anomalies have also surfaced during public tours of the museum. Glowing orbs of light and phantom mists not visible to the naked eye have appeared on film when later developed. One woman claims that while filming a recent visit to the museum with her Sony digital camcorder, she may have captured one of these unexplainable events. Upon reviewing her footage several days later, she was shocked as an ethereal-like cloud came into the frame and passed right through her husband's body without his seeming awareness. The cloud then floated through a wall leading to a small, dark theater showing films on the legacy of President John F. Kennedy.

Finally, there are some that claim that to witness the dark figure for yourself, you don't even have to be in the museum. Simply stand outside in roughly the spot that the first bullets struck the President and gaze up into the infamous window from which the assassin marked his target for death. There you'll see a dark hazy figure staring down at you, just as Kennedy's killer must have those many years ago. Make no excuses however; the sniper's nest window is inaccessible to the living from inside the museum, making the dark figure staring back at you that much more of a mystery.

Many of those encountering the phantom of the museum have come to believe that it belongs to the accused assassin himself, Lee Harvey Oswald—who they surmise is now cursed to wander the site for eternity, regretting the crimes he committed in life. Some theories among paranormal researchers suggest that powerful emotions such as regret, sadness, or anger can act as an anchor to keep a spirit earthbound to a particular location. Until these spirits can find a way to release the weighty emotional baggage trapping them in the material world, they are doomed to haunt those places once familiar to them in life.

Conspiracy Theory

Could the spirit of Lee Harvey Oswald now roam the former Texas School Book Depository, caught in a terrible past that will never leave him?

There are some conspiracy theorists that argue Oswald was innocent of the crimes stacked against him and that he may have acted as the fall guy for something much bigger.

The infamous "Sniper's Nest." *Courtesy of the Sixth Floor Museum.*

Nothing perhaps displays this point more eloquently than a plaque outside the building itself, which reads, "On Nov. 22, 1963, the building gained national notoriety when Lee Harvey Oswald allegedly shot and killed President John F. Kennedy from the sixth floor window as the presidential motorcade passed the site." To accentuate the point, the word "allegedly" has been crudely underlined by someone.

Unfortunately, Lee Harvey Oswald was never given the chance to defend himself in a court of law. On November 24, 1963, while being transferred from the city to the county jail Oswald was shot and killed by Jack Ruby, a local night club owner with rumored ties to organized crime. Oswald was pronounced dead at Parkland Memorial Hospital at 1:07 PM, just a few minutes after Kennedy a few days before.

Ruby in turn was convicted in the murder of Oswald and sentenced to death in a trial ending in March of 1964. The verdict was then overturned on appeal in the fall of 1966, but while awaiting a second trial, he succumbed to lung cancer and died.

They say the shadows still haunt the Sixth Floor Museum; flitting around corners and filling the empty places before dashing away again. If you're lucky, and your eyes are just quick enough, you might just spot the figure doomed to haunt these halls of history—himself a victim of the events that occurred that unseasonably warm day on November 22, 1963.

The Sixth Floor Museum
411 Elm Street
Dallas, Texas 75202
Phone: 214.747.6660
Web: www.jfk.org

Do Not Disturb

The Hotel Lawrence.

Quite often in the middle of the night
you can hear them coming up and down the stairs,
but there's no one there.

—Anonymous employee
of the Hotel Lawrence

It begins as a subtle noise tugging you out of a heavy sleep. The hotel room is dark and only a few of its features are visible in the moonlight pouring through the window. The noise grows louder, becoming a harsh knocking sound at the door. You look over at the digital clock on the night stand. The glowing numbers reveal that it's 1:30 am. The knocking continues more frantically now. Someone is at your door.

Getting out of bed, you stumble across the floor, noticing for the first time how hot the room is. Wiping sweat from your brow, you make a mental note to complain about the air conditioner being broken. That is, after you find out who's knocking at your door so late at night? The knocking continues with more urgency. You reach for the handle and cautiously open the door to find a woman standing in the hallway dressed in a bathrobe and slippers. Right away you know that something is wrong by the worried look on her face.

"Please…can you help me?" she asks nervously wringing her hands together.

Then, in the blink of an eye, she's gone—simply vanished into thin air. Bewildered by the encounter, you stick your head out into the corridor, but all that remains are shadows and silence. With the hair now standing up on the back of your neck, you quickly shut the door again. This time you make doubly sure to bolt and chain every lock on the frame. Resolving to report the disturbance to management first thing in the morning, you slip back between the sheets. Maybe it was just a dream, you tell yourself as you close your eyes. That's when the knocking begins again.

Welcome to the Hotel Lawrence

Located on South Houston Street in downtown Dallas next to the historic West End, the hotel stands just across the street from the George Allen Courthouse. Built in 1925, the ten-story kaki and cream-colored structure was primarily intended to serve rail customers and other visitors to the city of Dallas. During the prohibition of the 20s and 30s it gained more than its share of colorful history with an illegal gambling casino on the second floor that attracted everyone from bootleggers to card sharks.

Over the years, the old place would change hands and names many times. It was first known as the Scott Hotel; then in the 1930s, it was renamed Hotel Lawrence, and later it became the Paramount Hotel. When the Maryland-based hotel company, Magna Hospitality Group took over in 2000, they rechristened it Hotel Lawrence once more.

After four million dollars in renovations, the interior was redesigned with a European-boutique style in mind that promised intimate rooms and personalized service. The hotel became so successful that in recent years it has been named "Best Hotel Deal in Dallas" by *D Magazine*.

After speaking at length with the General Manager, Sebron Hood III, I learned that in the eighty-two years since it was first constructed, it has gained a reputation for more than just comfort and good service. Many have come to believe that the ghosts of former guests who died during their stay there haunt the hotel.

Visitors and staff alike have reported a wide range of paranormal activity from the sound of invisible footsteps echoing through the lobby late at night to a spirit that resists anyone opening the door to room 807 unless they first say, "move over smiley."

Eager to help in anyway he could, Mr. Hood invited me to come and see for myself what was happening in the hotel and offered me free run of the place for one night. An offer such as this is a rarity in my line of work and just couldn't be passed up. Given the size and scope of the 118-room hotel, I knew I would need help on this one and so enlisted the aide of fellow researchers, Carl Hullett, Barry Turnage, and Teresa Griffith of DFW Ghost Hunters.

The Thing in the Basement

The day of the investigation, we arrived late in order to avoid as many of the guests as we could. No need to attract attention to ourselves if we didn't have to. After checking in with the front desk, we began setting up operations in the basement using cameras and motion detectors. This area is well known by employees for doors opening and closing by themselves, cold spots, disembodied voices, and strange

Room 807 "Smiley's room."

feelings that they are being watched. On more than one occasion, staff members reported that heavy laundry carts in the basement moved toward them as if being pushed by an invisible force. In addition, the figure of a man dressed in black has been seen roaming the underground corridors of the place appearing and disappearing at free will.

For many of the hotel staff, the basement is a place they just don't go down into if they don't have to. For us, however, it would be the first stop and also the first of many strange events to transpire that night.

Our first sign of unusual activity occurred while Carl and I were taking instrument readings from the equipment. Suddenly, one of the storage room doors began opening by itself. Calling out in surprise, I raised my camera to capture the event, but when I depressed the shutter button the camera simply went dead. Checking it, I discovered that the new batteries I'd placed in it just before the investigation began had been drained of their power.

This is not as uncommon as you would think and researchers have long reported strange equipment malfunctions or power drainage when spirits are thought to be present. Some theorize that when a spirit is trying to manifest itself, energy is drawn from the environment around it—that includes camera batteries, too. Either way, if I stood any chance of gathering proof this night, I would have to be far quicker on the draw.

Haunting of the Tenth Floor

After several hours of further monitoring in the basement, we agreed to move to the hotel's tenth floor, which many claim is a hotbed of ghostly activity. Numerous guests staying on this floor have complained that they were awakened in the middle of the night by the sound of someone knocking on their doors. When they answer, they are confronted by a frantic woman still dressed in her bathrobe and slippers asking for their help. Before the startled guest can respond, however, she vanishes right before their eyes.

During the long course of the building's history, several suicides have been said to occur in rooms on this floor. One is attributed to a woman staying in room 1009, who jumped to her death from the hotel's roof; the other is linked to a former congressman who took his own life in room 1015, the Presidential Suite.

Since the congressman's death, strange calls are forwarded to the front desk from the room late at night when no one is staying there. When answered by staff, the only sound heard is a loud static-like noise from the other end. It was in the Presidential Suite that we set up shop next, and also when we realized that we had left the camera's batteries back in the basement.

One Scary Ride

Volunteering for the job, Carl and I left to retrieve the necessary equipment from the basement. It was during the return trip, however, that we ran into the trouble. Previously that night, we'd learned through interviewing hotel staff that precisely one week earlier at 1:30 am, the hotel elevator became stuck between floors. This left a number of guests trapped inside before help arrived.

Following the incident, a maintenance team inspected the elevator, but was unable to discern what caused the malfunction. That is until it was discovered that someone or something had pushed a large folding table into the elevator shaft from the basement access way. The staff was at a loss to explain how such an incident could have occurred. After all, the one entrance to the basement was locked at that hour and a subsequent review of security tapes showed no one entering or exiting the area all night.

It should have been no great surprise then, that while traveling back to the 10th floor to rejoin our team, the elevator ground to a halt between floors, effectively trapping us inside. The time was exactly 1:30 am.

Eventually, help did arrive and we were successfully extracted, but as we climbed the long winding staircase to the top, I couldn't help but get the feeling that something was trying to stop us from proceeding with our investigation.

Room 1015

Back in room 1015, we began rigging the place with sound recorders and night vision cameras for an experiment. Sitting in a rough circle with the lights off, we attempted to communicate with any spirits that might be present by addressing a series of questions aloud. Simple things really, like, "Are there any spirits present tonight?" or "Please tell us what your name is?" Audio equipment then records the session, filtering it through a computer terminal designed to spot potential EVPs (electronic voice phenomena). If there was something willing to communicate with us, it would be up to our instruments to pick it up. It was during one such EVP session that we did get a response—only it didn't happen the way we anticipated it would.

An (EMF) electromagnetic field meter positioned on the bed nearby to measure possible fluctuations in the magnetic fields caused by spirits suddenly began to sound its alarm. Barry Turnage, leaning over the device to measure the data, began calling out measurements when just like that, the EMF meter moved by itself. Not far mind you, a mere inch or two, but just enough to send us a clear message—we were not alone.

The sun was just rising as we wearily packed the equipment up and piled it into the truck. The night had certainly been a lively one and exhaustion was written on every face. The hotel had no doubt lived up to its reputation and left us a lot to ponder for the drive home.

Hotel Lawrence is a place of comfort and hospitality where the staff goes to great lengths to ensure your stay will be a pleasant one. Nonetheless, it's also a place where the spirits of former guests long passed have refused to check out. If you do decide to visit, make sure to ask the always-friendly staff to share a few of their ghost stories with you. If you stay the night (which I certainly suggest), you might want to hang your "Do Not Disturb" sign on the door before going to bed.

Just remember, whatever you do, if someone knocks at 1:30 am—don't answer the door; or do, depending on your ghostly curiosity.

The Hotel Lawrence
302 South Houston Street
Dallas, Texas 75202
Phone: 214.761.9090
Web: www.hotellawrencedallas.com

The Town that Time Forgot

The Millermore Mansion at Old City Park.

The air was filled with phantoms,
wandering hither and thither in restless haste,
and moaning as they went.

—Charles Dickens,
"A Christmas Carol"

Over the years, a ghost hunter will count themselves lucky if they manage to scrape together a handful of places they believe to be truly haunted. After all, haunted houses don't grow on trees. Yet near the very heart of Dallas's downtown district lies an unusual public attraction that may prove otherwise. The Dallas Heritage Village at Old City Park is a town that time seems to have forgotten all about—where the ghosts said to wander its buildings far out number the living. When I first received the call to join Joel Thomas from *CBS Channel 11 News* and other local ghost hunters on an investigation of the site one chilly October evening, I knew from the start I was in for a wild night.

Heritage Village

Entering the Heritage Village on South Harwood Street is like taking a seat in one of H. G. Wells's time machines and flipping the switch backwards. The thirteen acres of what was once the city's oldest public park are now full of lush flowerbeds and shaded wooded paths. Crisscrossing the pastoral scenery are cobbled streets and a bewildering assortment of homes and businesses taken from the pages of history itself. Here visitors to the park can find an eclectic mixture of architectural styles ranging from simple log cabins and shotgun houses to the lavishness of the Queen Ann homes from the late 1800s. Interspersed with these little marvels are businesses as well, including a print shop, bank, general store, blacksmith, Methodist church, school house, train depot, and to round it all off, its very own hotel. Each of these buildings is an authentic structure taken from locations all over north Texas and lovingly restored to their former glories.

Over 25,000 historical artifacts, from 1840 to 1910, enhance each building as costumed volunteers roam the streets demonstrating various crafts and trades such as weaving or candle making. In fact, the village is considered a "living museum" and visitors are encouraged to interact with volunteers, who keeping with character, share stories and answer questions about times far removed from our own.

The Dallas Heritage Village is a surreal place, where the smell of wood-burning stoves and the banging of the blacksmith's hammer contrast sharply with the city's skyscrapers. Yet as Hal Simon, the museum's curator, would warn, as the team unloaded its equipment in the parking lot, it's also a place inhabited with ghosts.

Lucy Jane Browder was the first to purchase the land that the park now sits on in the late 1840s. Before that, it was a camping ground for native tribes of Caddoan moving through the area hunting buffalo. Sometime between 1876 and 1885, the city of Dallas assumed the property and converted it into the city park. Built as an oasis for the citizens of Dallas, its grounds were landscaped with colorful flowers and winding walkways. As the park grew in stride with the city, tennis courts were added, along with a swimming pool, and eventually, even a small zoo.

It wasn't until the 1960s, that the first of the village's historical buildings came to the park through a most unusual series of events. As the story goes, on February 18, 1966, a beautiful old antebellum mansion was scheduled for demolition. To protest its impending destruction, a group of local women gathered on its front steps and faced down the oncoming bulldozers.

Rather than risk a messy confrontation with the stubborn little group of protestors, workers turned off the machines and halted demolition. The ladies had won an important victory that day and followed their success by forming the Dallas County Heritage Society to prevent other historical home from falling prey to what nowadays is often called "progress."

The old mansion was taken apart brick by brick and later relocated to the city park where it finally found a safe haven. By 1976, more buildings were added to the park and suddenly, as if by magic, a small town began to grow in the middle of a bustling city.

The plan for the evening's hunt was simple. Once the park shut its gates for the night, museum officials would shuttle teams of ghost hunters around in golf carts to various buildings throughout the grounds. Once we started, I had to smile at the picture we cut. Can you imagine teams of ghost hunters flying down darkened streets past ancient buildings in golf carts loaded with electronic equipment?

The Mysterious Woman
of Millermore Mansion

Given the vast number of locations to choose from, we decided to narrow the search to only a handful of the park's most haunted buildings. Therefore, our first stop of the night led us to none other than the very structure that started it all—the Millermore Mansion.

Named for its owner, William Brown Miller, who began construction in 1855 for his wife Minerva Miller, the house took approximately six years to complete. Tragically, Minerva died soon after work began on the home and never lived to see its completion.

The spot Miller choose sat close to his original log cabin home, but Millermore would be nothing like it. Set in the Greek revival style popular with the affluent at the time, Miller filled it with luxurious furnishings that reflected his success. It must have been a sight to see rising above the tree line with its symmetrical façade and Doric portico at the front door. The stately Ionic columns of the front porch, which give it a distinctively southern character, were not added until 1912, however.

Since first coming to the park many years ago the mansion has been the scene of numerous reports surrounding the apparition of a mysterious woman. In most versions, she is spotted nervously pacing back and forth between the upstairs nursery and the master bedroom. Accounts go on to explain that although she seems not to notice the presence of others, witnesses to the event are often struck with overwhelming sensations of fear and nausea.

Deborah Lister, the Office Administrator, commented that she, along with others, have also seen the ghost peering out at them from an upstairs window as they strolled down the mansion's lane. Each time, the spectral figure appears as a woman in a light-colored dress from the 1880s, with her hands clasped in front of her. Details of the figure are reported to stand out clearly in the window with all but the exception of the face, which seems to fade into nothingness. Although the identity of the ghost is yet unknown, its clothes bear a striking resemblance to those worn by Minerva Miller in an old daguerreotype found by park officials.

Other unexplained events have transpired in the mansion that are believed to be the work of the phantom. Objects move around by themselves when no one is looking and rooms on the second floor are prone to suffering dramatic temperature shifts for no apparent reason. So frequent are the encounters with the agitated spirit that Curator Hal Simon is fond of remarking that when opening the building each morning, he calls out to announce his presence. Seems Hal and the ghost of the Millermore have a mutual agreement; he won't scare it, as long as it doesn't scare him.

The Shy Ghost of Katy

With these stories in mind, we canvassed the mansion from top to bottom with cameras and audio equipment before climbing back into our golf carts, now christened "ghost carts," and made our way to the village's train depot. This structure was originally built in Fate, Texas, around 1886, and is typical of the board and batten style used by the Missouri-Kansas-Texas Railroad, also known as the Katy. Its plain exterior and simple rooms, however, have gained quite the reputation among park staff for housing the spirit of a very shy ghost.

Those that have run into him late at night while locking up claim to see the weathered old face of a black man peeking out at them from behind one of the storage room doors. Subsequent searches of the buildings and closets reveal nothing, but the storage area was once the *black's only* section of the station when segregation still ruled the south. Unlike some of the park's other ghostly inhabitants this spirit seems more inquisitive than threatening and some of the staff surmise that he's just waiting on his train—a train that will never come.

The Train Depot at Old City Park.

It was here that investigators took some of the night's first anomalous photographs. Reviewing my own pictures from the storage area later on showed a small band of light weaving a long tail in and out of the frame.

Murder
at the Thompson and Knight Law Office

By now, hours had passed in that excitingly subdued way that they will on an investigation, and one location remained yet to be explored. In the interest of time, some of the team returned to Millermore Mansion for further testing, while I and a small band marched down the street to the Thompson and Knight Law Office.

This building, with its decidedly box-like shape of red brick, was constructed in 1906, on the corner of Oak and Nussbaumer in east Dallas. It was actually a meat market run by Italian and Hispanic immigrants, but once relocated to the park, officials thought it would make a better addition if refurbished as a law office.

The Law Office at Old City Park.

Despite all of the grand buildings that have come to find a home in City Park, it's perhaps this quaint little neighborhood store that holds the greatest mystery. As newspapers from the period recount, one day in 1929, two men entered the store and gunned its proprietor down in what was labeled a "mob style" execution. The assailants fled on foot taking nothing with them and were never brought to justice. What witnesses there were to the shooting were reluctant to come forward, and to this day, the crime remains unsolved.

Since its relocation to the park, volunteers tasked with working in the law office have shied away from the building after only a few days with complaints of nausea, dizziness, and depression. As if difficulty staffing the law office weren't enough, an even bigger problem involves the building's security system. Although the internal alarm system has been replaced many times over the years, it's often triggered in the middle of the night as if an intruder has broken in. Oddly enough, each time park security is dispatched to the scene, they find little more than an empty building with no explanation as to who or what set the alarm off.

It was in this very building that I too came to experience what so many of the park's volunteers have encountered in the past. While snapping photographs of the exact spot where the storeowner collapsed in a pool of his own blood, an uncomfortable sensation began creeping over me. Insidiously, a sickening feeling started to rise from the pit of my stomach. I tried to ignore it and continue working, but the longer I stayed, the stronger it grew, until an almost embarrassing sense of panic overwhelmed me.

Excusing myself from the rest of the team, I stepped out and into the cool night air. Almost immediately, I began to feel better and it seemed as if a great weight had been lifted from me. If I thought that it was just me, however, I was wrong, and before long, I was joined by other members of the team, each reporting similar symptoms of their own.

Later, while digging into the history of the place more thoroughly, I discovered an interesting fact that shared a striking similarity to my physical unease in that building. The storeowner gunned down that day in 1929, died from bullet wounds to the stomach; a death that to this day continues to play itself out over and over again. I have experienced residual impressions at the scene of a haunting such as this in the past, but never so strongly.

With morning fast approaching and a lingering feeling of heaviness after working in the law office, the group packed up and called it a night. Riding past the darkened homes and business that make up the Heritage Village, I couldn't help but wonder if the spirits that lived within weren't staring out at us from behind the deeper blackness of the windowpanes. Maybe they were just waiting for us to leave so they could take to their cobbled streets again. Maybe to them we were the ghosts, flitting by in the night, haunting their buildings, and making a ruckus—something distantly familiar to them, yet no longer of their world. After all, sometimes in this business it's hard to tell whose haunting whom.

I still return to the Dallas Heritage Village at Old City Park on occasion just to wander its streets and peer into its windows. As a writer and historian, I love the thrill it gives me of being transported back into the past. Every home, every business here, oozes with stories. If you go there yourself, don't be shy about asking the park staff to recount some of their favorite ghost stories for you. As a historical and academic organization, park officials take their job very seriously, but oh, how they do love their ghosts.

The Dallas Heritage Village in Old City Park
1515 South Harwood Street
Dallas, Texas 75215
Phone: 214.421.5141
Web: www.oldcitypark.org

A German Ghost Story

Entrance to the Sons of Hermann Hall.

Come down some afternoon…
and I guarantee you'll hear or see something—
footsteps upstairs, chairs moving—
and nobody there.

—Jo Nicodemus,
Manager of the Sons of Hermann Hall

G ermany has always had a deep and abiding love affair with its ghosts. From its dark, impenetrable forests to the lofty ruins of its ancient castes, ghosts can be found throughout the country's folklore. In fact, even our own English word for ghosts can be traced back to the German term *geist*. Why then are we concerned with the ghosts of a land over 5,000 miles away you ask? Because many of the German immigrants settling in the plains and hills of central Texas came to the region with more than just an oxcart and dreams of a new life. They also brought with them a belief in the supernatural that helped to color the tales and traditions of Texas. Keeping this in mind then, the tale you are about to hear is as much a German ghost story as it is a Texan.

The Sons of Hermann

In the 1840s, harsh social and economic conditions in Germany, coupled with the news of land to be had in Texas, left many dreaming of a fresh start on the Texas frontier. To capitalize on the growing movement westward, a group of German nobles formed the Association for the Protection of German Immigrants in 1842.

The *Verein*, as it was called in German, obtained an immense land grant in central Texas totaling 38,800,000 acres. Prospective settlers were promised 320 acres of land per family to relocate as well as transportation, houses, churches, roads, hospitals and all the provisions needed to make a go of it. The *Verein* however, was not as concerned with protecting immigrants as they were with alleviating overcrowding in rural Germany and obtaining a new source wealth and power. As a result, many German newcomers perished from starvation, epidemics, and other hardships along the route. Those that did survive settled in cities such as Dallas, Houston, and San Antonio or established towns like New Braunfels or Fredericksburg in the rugged Texas hill country. In the end, the *Verein's* dreams of new glory and riches quickly turned into financial ruin, but the venture did serve to bring thousands of German peasants to Texas between 1844 and 1847.

In 1861, two of those German immigrants founded the Order of the Sons of Hermann in the State of Texas. As a fraternal benefit society, the order pledged itself to the preservation of the German culture in Texas. The first grand lodge began in San Antonio, but as the ranks swelled with new members, other lodges sprang up throughout the state.

To better identify with their cultural heritage and instill bravery and steadfastness in their brethren, the order took its name from a first-century German folk hero, Hermann the Defender. Hermann was famous for uniting the German tribes and defeating three Roman legions at the battle of Teutoburg Forest in 9 A.D. After outwitting and outfighting his Roman opponents, he was unceremoniously murdered by members of his own tribe who feared his growing power. To this day, many Germans see Hermann as something of a "George Washington" figure and monuments to the fallen hero stand wherever large concentrations of German descendents exist.

By 1910, there were four such lodges established in the city of Dallas. In an effort to pool their resources, the lodges banned together and purchased a piece of property on the eastern edge of town known as Deep Ellum, which it turns out is a corruption of "Deep Elm."

The simple two-story box-like structure erected one year later became known as the Sons of Hermann Hall. Members, who had to be of German descent, met regularly at the hall to listen and dance to polkas, drink beer, bowl, and speak in their native German tongue. During the summers, children attended classes in German language, history, and culture. Yet the order, like many others (such as the Freemasons and Knights of Columbus), was not without its own set of mysteries. Meetings were held in German to discourage spies, peepholes were installed on the doors, and to gain entrance, you had to know the secret handshake.

Since that time, Hermann Hall and the German order that founded it have adapted well to the twenty-first century. Although the order remains one of the nation's oldest fraternal benefit societies, the hall has become a popular venue for live music, and membership is no longer regulated to those of German descent.

The neighborhood as well has seen more than its share of change over the years. Deep Ellum started in 1884, as a commercial zone filled with factories and warehouses. By the 1920s, the streets were alive, not with the drone of usual commerce, but with the melodic sounds jazz trumpets and the blues guitars. Musicians such as "Blind" Lemon Jefferson, Huddie "Leadbelly" Ledbetter, and Besse Smith played at clubs on the strip with names like The Harlem and The Palace.

During the 1960s and 1970s, the area attracted a large number of artists looking for cheap housing and studio space. The neighborhood began to deteriorate and its unlit streets gained the reputation for being a dangerous place after dark. Despite a well-deserved face lift with new streets, lights, and parking in the 1980s, the area continues to struggle with a high crime rate. Gone are the wailing jazz clubs of the 1920s, replaced with crowded bars, pulsing night clubs, and tattoo parlors.

Spirits of the Hall

Regardless of the language, Hermann Hall has for years echoed with the hushed tales of the ghosts said to inhabit it. Jo Nicodemus, long time manager of the historic building, remembers all too well her own chance encounters with the spirits of the hall.

One night, while conducting a board meeting, she and over a dozen members heard the sounds of children yelling and playing in the next room. Thinking that it was far too late for children to be in the building, one member rose to investigate, but after a careful search, no trace of them could be found.

At other times, the harsh disembodied voice of a man has been overheard as if it were scolding children. For those long-time members who have heard the sound, many recognize it as belonging to a former caretaker named Louie Bernardt. Louie was well known for his impatience with children playing in the hall and often yelled at them for it.

On another occasion, Jo Nicodemus relates that while sitting in her office with another member finishing up the day's paperwork, a man slowly walked by her open doorway. Knowing the building was closed at this hour, the two jumped up to follow, but after yet another fruitless search, the pair concluded that they were alone in the building.

In time this wouldn't be the only phantom to reveal itself to eyewitnesses. On one memorable occasion, an episode of *Walker, Texas Ranger* was being filmed on the site. After a long day of shooting, the extras had gathered in the bar to relax with a few cold beers. Suddenly, the room grew very cold as a lavishly dressed wedding couple entered the room arm and arm. The man appeared to be wearing a top hat and tuxedo coat while the woman was dressed in an extravagant wedding gown. At first, everyone who glanced up thought they were movie extras—after all, no one dresses like that anymore. Yet, as they glided through the room and disappeared into the back corridor, it suddenly dawned on the patrons that something was wrong.

Several of the braver drinkers set off to find the couple but returned a short time later. Yep, you guessed it, the couple was no where to be found.

Other events have transpired in the hall leaving witnesses with a decidedly uneasy feeling. Doors are known to open and then slam shut, even after being locked tight. Pictures framed on the walls have toppled off without explanation and many frequenting the hall get the eerie feeling they're being watched.

On more than one occasion, employees have complained that after cleaning up for the night, they returned the next morning to find their work undone and the place in complete disarray. One bartender even recounts an experience he claims he will never forget after locking up one night. Just as he was driving away, he looked back and watched a light on the second-story flick on. Turning back he reentered the building and raced up the stairs to the second floor. Nevertheless, by the time he reached the second-story landing, the light was off again.

To help get a better feel for the place, I contacted Dawn Marshall, a paranormal researcher known to rely on her psychic abilities to aide her investigations. Dawn is someone who knows Hermann Hall all too well and has visited it on numerous occasions attempting to contact the spirits she believes still reside there.

During one session Dawn wandered about the building seeking to get a feel for the place psychically. In the upstairs ballroom, she encountered the first of the building's ghosts. Upon entering the room, a mental image came to her of two brothers dressed in clothing from an older time period. They seemed upset about the way the building looked nowadays and were trying to impress upon her that at one time it was quite nice and the scene of many elegant parties.

Bowling for Ghosts

Despite the spirits of the ballroom, it would fall upon the downstairs bowling alley to provide the most unsettling experience. Even entering the room proved difficult and she immediately sensed that bad things occurred there long ago. Her first sensation was of a shortness of breath as if something was wrong with her chest. This sometimes happens, she explained, when a spirit wants to communicate what they went through.

Moving to an open doorway leading to an outside parking lot, Dawn began to feel like someone was standing next to her watching and worrying. A second mental image then flashed through her head of two men fist fighting, followed by one of them being shot in the chest. Since then, Dawn has returned time and again, and although she believes there is nothing evil or threatening about the place, she does feel that there is a lot of spirit activity.

When dealing with psychics in the past I have more often than not found their impressions hard to validate in light of the evidence. Imagine my surprise then, after some good old-fashioned detective work, I stumbled upon an interesting article in the *Dallas Daily Times Herald* dated July 6, 1897.

It seems that, according to the article, William Hardbrecht shot a man named Walter Stover on the street outside the building. The altercation started as a fistfight between the two, but when Stover got the better of Hardbrecht, the second man pulled a gun and shot Stover in the chest. Although a large crowd had gathered to watch, no one was willing to talk to authorities about the incident.

Is this proof positive that a link exists between the living and the dead? Well perhaps not, but it hardly seems something you can chalk up to mere coincidence either. If you're one of those adventurous souls bent on finding out the truth for themselves, however, then I suggest you pay the hall a visit some night. Once you get there, just saddle up to the bar and ask the person next to you about the ghosts roaming the place. You're bound to get an earful. When they're done weaving their tales, thank them politely and shake their hand. After all, you need to make sure you haven't just spent the last half hour speaking to a phantom.

If you do decide to wander away from the well-lit common areas into the building's darker rooms, you may want to brush up on your German first—just in case an eerie voice calls out to you from the darkness, "Sprechen Sie Deutsche?"

The Sons of Hermann Hall
3414 Elm Street
Dallas, Texas 75371
Phone: 214.747.4422
Web: www.sonsofhermann.com

Wakening the Dead

Snuffer's Restaurant.

Sometimes a meal can haunt you for days...
one way or another.

—Dotty Griffith,
Restaurant Critic

On Lower Greenville Avenue, northeast of Dallas's downtown section is one of the oldest entertainment quarters in the city. From hip boutiques and eclectic shops to cozy bars and ethnic restaurants spaced between 1920s, bungalows, the street comes alive each night as locals and visitors alike flock to the area.

Lower Greenville, as it's called, is also home to the city's best burger joint, Snuffer's Restaurant. Here you can find a half pound of ground chuck grilled to perfection, topped with fresh lettuce and tomatoes, and dripping in hot cheddar cheese. If that doesn't get your juices going, then just try their legendary cheddar fries with aged cheddar cheese melted over hand-cut Idaho potatoes. Wash that down with a tall frosty glass of Shiner Bock and you have a meal guaranteed to clog your arteries, but man what a way to go.

Snuffer's has gained such a reputation that it's appeared in local and national food publications including the *Dallas Morning News*, who named it as having the "Best Burger" in town. Although you can find numerous mouth-watering delights on their menu, one thing you won't find advertised are the spirits that come with your meal.

Pat Snuffer first opened his restaurant at the corner of Longview Street and Greenville Avenue on June 28, 1978. It began as a small affair consisting of a one-room building capable of holdings up to only fifty-five customers. To save on costs, Pat furnished the place with tables, booths, and chairs he made himself. Three others helped finish out the rest of the interior, and before long, the restaurant was serving up burgers as fast as hungry customers could scarf them down.

After about a year, things were running so smoothly Pat decided to expand the business into an adjacent section of the building that has come to be called "The Back Room," which doubled the seating capacity. Renovations to connect the two sections began in 1979, and almost immediately, so did the haunting.

The Back Room Spectre

Pat was the first to encounter the phantom late one night after closing in January of 1979, recalling that the figure appeared before him as if it were draped in a black sheet and, after gliding past him, disappeared into thin air.

At first, he was reluctant to share the experience with anyone, afraid they would think him crazy and that it would hurt his business. But since that night, the dark specter

Hallway leading to the "Back Room."

has been seen repeatedly by both the customers and staff. Each time it appears in the same place—a narrow L-shaped corridor connecting the older building with the newer addition to the south. Eye witnesses report that it moves slowly through the hallway from "The Back Room" to the original portion of the building; vanishing just as it enters the main dinning area.

The identity of the specter is unclear, but two stories similar in nature persist that may point us in the right direction. Both originate from a time before the restaurant, when the building was home to a rough and tumble bar frequented by bikers.

The first tells the story of a biker set on reforming his ways. The tale goes that this biker made a promise to his girlfriend that he would stop frequenting the place and give up his old rowdy buddies.

Coming to the bar one last time to say goodbye to his pals, a fight broke out with a rival biker gang. Caught in the middle of the ensuing melee, he was stabbed in the hallway and managed to crawl outside where he bled to death on the sidewalk.

The second tells of a man who collapsed in the hallway from a fatal heart attack, his body wedged in the bathroom door, effectively holding it open.

Regardless of the truth of the matter, something now haunts this area of the restaurant refusing to leave. All of the sightings describe the specter as a dark hazy figure with no distinct features and no sign that it is aware of its surroundings or of other people.

Other Ghostly Shenanigans

Other apparitions have been reported as well, with many of the occurrences transpiring after the place has closed for the night. One waitress reported that after closing, she entered the main restaurant section to find a woman sitting atop the cigarette machine. Knowing the placed was locked tight, she went to get the manager, but when they returned together, the woman was gone and no trace of her presence could be found.

Other employees claim to have felt the touch of an invisible hand on their shoulders while going about their duties or have heard their names whispered in a harsh sounding voice three times when they were alone.

In one of the more ominous sightings, some recount seeing a pair of glowing red eyes peering out at them from under table number seven in the dining section.

For the most part however, much of the phenomena seems to appear mischievous rather than threatening, as if the spirits of Snuffer's delighted in playing otherworldly jokes on their unsuspecting victims. After hours, while trying to wipe off tables, the ashtrays and other glassware move about when the staff has their backs turned. Sometimes the objects move from one table to another across a space of almost seven or eight feet. At other times, green hanging lamps in the dining room begin swinging in unison. When the staff decided to try and reproduce the anomalies to prove it had a natural cause, they were unable to, despite their best efforts.

Then Came the Ghost Hunters

On September 20, 1998, members of the Southwest Ghost Hunters Association decided to pay the place a visit and see if they could capture evidence of the elusive spirits. While searching the infamous back corridor, which seems a hotspot for one of the spirits, the EMF meters they were using to measure disturbances in the magnetic fields associated with ghosts went crazy. To further deepen the mystery, they reported an odd mist in a number of the photographs taken by their team of the hallway.

Following in their footsteps I too decided to visit the restaurant and see what spirits I could dig up. Unfortunately, I wasn't as lucky and none of my photographs revealed anything. I did get a lot of strange looks though. Can you imagine sitting down to a great meal with your friends and some guy walking by sweeping the air in front of him with an odd gadget complete with flashing lights and beeping noises?

It is interesting to note however that the haunting began after renovations commenced back in 1979. In the paranormal world, this happens more than you would think and follows a classic pattern seen time and again by researchers. It goes something like this: Someone moves into a nice location **and e**verything is quiet until they begin to renovate the place to suit their tastes. Then boom—instant haunting; almost as if the spirits resided in the place the entire time, but in a state of dormancy. Following all of the banging and sawing, they suddenly awake and are not too happy about being so rudely disturbed. Perhaps the spirits just want to keep things the way they remembered them in life; either way, the owners of Snuffer's woke something up one day in 1979, and it hasn't rested since.

Whether you prefer a good ghost story or a great burger you'll find both at Snuffer's Restaurant.

Snuffer's Restaurant
3526 Greenville Avenue
Dallas, Texas 75206
Phone: 214.826.6850
Web: www.snuffers.com

The Ghost in the Machine

That's the problem with ghosts:
they only appear to other people.

—Joanna St. Angelo,
Director of the Sammons Art Center

J ust a few blocks north of the city's downtown district, with its stunning blend of historic landmarks mixing eclectically with modern towers of glass and steel, is a section of Dallas known as Oak Lawn. As one of the wealthier areas of the city its streets seem to literally sprout upscale townhouses and condos amid tree-lined roads and parks echoing with the sounds of little league games. Wandering through the streets, it's easy to imagine that Oak Lawn has always been a model of prosperity for the sprawling metropolis of Dallas. Yet under the façade of boutique stores and smiling pedestrians walking their dogs, hides a unique and tragic history and as we're about to see—a ghost or two.

On May 26, 1908, the Trinity River, which borders the western edge of the city, welled up from its confining banks and flooded much of the area. Although the river had periodically escaped its boundaries in the past, the deluge of 1908, was like nothing the city had seen before. For three days and three nights the city effectively lost its ability to operate leaving Dallas without power, communications, or access to rail lines.

Conditions were so dreadful in some areas that the *Dallas Herald Times* characterized the scene as "indescribable suffering." All told, five people died in the flood of 1908, with 4,000 losing their homes and millions in property damage. As the waters began to recede, a new horror replaced the devastation of the flood. Thousands of livestock drowned in the rushing waters of the river now

The Sammons Center for the Arts.

lay tossed in the tops of trees and roofs as the stench of decay filled the city. (Payne 1982, 119—155)

Despite the destruction Mother Nature visited on the city, citizens of Dallas just plain refused to give in. Reconstruction began immediately with improvements being made to bridges, roads, and levees along the river. Carcasses and other debris were swept from the streets, homes rebuilt, lives put back together, and a new pump station was built on higher ground in Oak Lawn.

The Turtle Creek Pump Station

Known as the Turtle Creek Pump Station, this public work was completed in 1909, and acted as the sole source of clean drinking water for the city until 1930. Designed by the prominent architectural firm of C. A. Gill and Sons, it was modeled in the fancifully ornate detailing of the Italianate style.

By 1930, the Pump Station became obsolete as more modern systems of water management were developed. With the pumps shut down after two decades of service, the building continued on, housing other functions of the Dallas Water Utility System.

In the early 1950s, portions of the south and west walls were destroyed to make way for improvements along Harry Hines Boulevard. The new configuration left the structure permanently altered in the unusual configuration visible today. Four years later, the Turtle Creek Pump Station was retired after many years of faithful service to the city of Dallas and, as a reward, it was abandoned.

For almost thirty years the station sat empty; falling prey to the ravages of time and neglect. Floors caved in, windows shattered, and rainwater coated the walls in long red streaks of rust and slime. The station became a place of windblown leaves, dripping water, and the occasional teenagers looking for a place to drink beer.

Even then rumors abound that something otherworldly walked the hollow shell of the old pump station. Perhaps it was the way that the shadows fell when the sun poured in through the broken windows or the sound of the wind whistling through the rafters, but many who ventured in into the ruins came to believe that something still lurked there.

Then on June 24, 1981, the Turtle Creek Pump Station was recognized as a historic landmark and the Sammons Center for the Arts Coalition formed with the purpose of restoring the crumbling landmark. After seven years of hard work and three million dollars, the old pump station reopened as the Sammons Center for the Arts. Now nonprofit arts organizations had a home for events, rehearsals, auditions, and meetings. At this time, as many as twelve different organizations use the facility including the Sammons Jazz Series and the Shakespeare Festival of Dallas. Today the former Turtle Creek Pump Station is one of the oldest public buildings in the city of Dallas.

Flirting With a Phantom

From the start of the building's new life as an arts center in 1988, many have noticed that some of the building's machinery acts as if it had a mind of its own. Most notable is the building's old elevator system. Employees locking up for the night often hear the elevator come to life and begin to transverse the floors on its own.

In the mornings as well, employees are sometimes greeted by the elevator doors opening for them as they approach. Those familiar with its quirky behavior believe it to be haunted by a ghost they refer to as Otis; a name taken from the company that built the center's elevator system. Another unusual pattern noticed by workers is that Otis seems to have a thing for the ladies. On some occasions, the elevator doors will open when a young, attractive woman walks by almost as if it were an invitation.

Otis's elevator.

Service crews maintaining the system have been called out many times over the years and asked to explain the odd mechanical behavior of the elevator. The motor has been rebuilt three times, a new jack installed, and over time, almost every part eventually replaced. Still, no one has yet to solve the mystery and the elevator continues its astonishing habits as before.

Yet if you think Otis has resigned himself to only haunting the elevator then you couldn't be farther from the truth. Witnesses to the strange events unfolding at the arts center have claimed to see his apparition roaming other parts of the building as well. Each time, he appears mostly to women and is described as a young man, wearing overalls, a jacket, and a workman's cap.

On one such occasion, a woman was working at her desk in the first floor office when she looked up from her stack of papers to find a man standing just a few feet away from her.

"I'll be right with you sir," she responded, before turning back down to the pressing work on her desk.

It was at that moment, to her shock and unease that she remembered the building was not open yet and still locked tight. Immediately she looked up again, but the man was gone. Enlisting the aide of another employee, the two searched the building, checking every door and window as they went, but the supposed intruder had disappeared as if in thin air.

During a similar encounter, another women reported that she was sitting at her desk listening to a CD of instrumental music while she worked. Before long, she began to notice a male voice singing softly along with the tune. Bewildered by the sound, she stopped the music and was greeted by a loud burst of laughter that filled the room. The unnerving part was, she was alone. Rushing over to a coworker in an office down the hall, she replayed the CD, which proved to contain neither the singing nor the laughter she heard earlier.

If Otis seemed to delight in the occasional song once in awhile, then he also proved to be quite a trickster. Paperwork, small objects, and other items that seem to catch his fancy are periodically known to disappear off the desks of office workers. Victims of his ghostly pranks are then dumbfounded when the items reappear days later in the exact location they vanished from in the first place.

Although his reputation for the ladies is well known around the arts center, that hasn't stopped him from appearing to a few men as well. While closing the building up for the night, a maintenance worker was making his rounds through the second-floor kitchen turning off lights when he heard a voice say "bye." Without thinking he responded "bye" as well and then in the heart beat that it took for the realization to set in, he stopped dead in his tracks. He was supposed to be alone.

Mustering his courage, he searched the building room by room turning on all of the lights once again, but like others before him, he found nothing more than an empty building.

Old timers from the area point to an incident many years back when the pump station was still in operation that may shed light on the identity of the playful ghost. Stories exist about a young man in his early twenties who was killed in the basement during an accident involving some of the station's machinery. After the tragedy, workers carefully avoided the basement claiming that it maintained a constant chilly presence and that they felt as if they were being watched all the time. During the restoration period of the 1980s, engineers determined that the basement was unusable due to water seepage and filled it in.

There was one exception—the elevator shaft.

Late Night Investigations

Recently, members of two north Texas ghost hunting teams, the Phantom Hunters and White Noise Investigations, entered the building to find out for themselves if the stories of a haunting were true. During their investigation, they experienced a number of anomalies that gave them pause for thought. The first occurred while conducting Electromagnetic Field (EMF) sweeps of the third floor. Just as they approached the elevator, it began to ascend from the floors below by itself. Reaching the third floor, it opened its doors for the astounded ghost hunters to reveal an empty compartment.

The second strange event of the evening happened while conducting audio recordings of the third-floor conference room. After a long series of questions designed to prompt the spirit into speaking, the team was just about to wrap things up when a series of hard knocks sounded on a nearby wooden table.

Although the teams left that night with little in the way of hard evidence to prove the case for a haunting, they did experience things that led them to believe that something uncanny was happening there.

The staff at the Sammons Center for the Arts doesn't seem to mind Otis much now that they have gotten used to him. In fact, some of the women are down right flattered by his ghostly attentions and whenever something comes up missing they are fond of calling out, "Okay Otis, joke's over, put it back."

There are some however, like Joanna St. Angelo, the Executive Director for the center, who express a bit of remorse whenever they speak of the ghost.

"I think he just gets lonely when the place is empty and there's no one here," she states wistfully.

The Sammons Center for the Arts
3630 Harry Hines Boulevard
Dallas, Texas 75219
Phone: 214.520.7788
Web: www.sammonsartcenter.org

The Long Road Home

Preston Road.

Preston Road today is older than the city of Dallas…
older than the state of Texas,
the Republic of Texas,
and even the United States of America.

—Mitchel Whitington,
"Ghosts of North Texas"

M ost of us live in a nine to five world, which has little to do with ghosts or the paranormal. Each morning we rise, beating our way through rush hour traffic to earn a living, only to turn around and sit through the same terrible mess on our way home again. Yet for some Dallas commuters' making their way home after a hard day at the office, the paranormal becomes all too real.

When I first heard that phantoms were being reported along a busy section of Preston Road, I knew this was something I needed to see for myself. Little did I know, however, that this investigation was one that would place me dangerously closer to the spirit world than I had ever come before. In fact, this time I almost became a ghost myself.

An Ancient Pathway

For anyone who thinks the ghosts of Dallas are scary, then I challenge you to try evening rush hour along some of its more congested stretch of roads. Preston Road itself is one such hectic drive; beginning around the city's Highland Park area, it shoots straight as an arrow to the northern suburbs of Plano, Frisco, and beyond. More of an Indianapolis 500 Speedway really, it carries vast numbers of commuters back and fourth between their homes on the outskirts of Dallas and the daily grind of work downtown. Yet most of the drivers who travel this difficult route each day never realize the centuries worth of history they're speeding over, nor perhaps of the mystery that lies just beneath its pavement.

Preston Road was originally a pre-Columbian trade route winding its way through central Texas, with its rolling hills and spring-fed rivers, all the way to what has today become St. Louis, Missouri. Little is known is known of the early people who inhabited the area before the Europeans arrived. What we do know is that eventually a powerful tribe of Shawnee began using the ancient track while moving from the southern regions of the state to areas in the north.

By 1838, the budding young Republic of Texas decided that it needed a road from its capital in Austin to the Red River Territory. So two years later, the Republic commissioned Colonel W. G. Cooke to conduct a survey expedition along what had come to be called the Shawnee Trail. In October of 1840, with preparations finished,

Colonel Cooke crossed the Trinity River on a march northward, which finally ended at a military outpost near the Red River named Fort Preston. Between that time and the coming of the railroad three decades later, Cooke's historic route became known as Preston Trail.

Preston Road, as it was later officially named, served as the principal path for immigration into northern Texas in the following years. Settlers crossed the Red River just below its confluence with the Washita River at the Rock Bluff Crossing and followed the road to its southern terminus at the settlement of Cedar Springs, now part of downtown Dallas. Cattlemen also used the road to drive huge herds of Texas longhorns to railheads in the north for shipment to Kansas meat markets. These drovers gave the road names of their own, including the Sedalia Trial, the Kansas Trail, and simply "The Trail."

Nowadays those early cattlemen and pioneers traveling the same road won't recognize what it's become. Gone are the expansive plains filled with stubborn prairie grass, Juniper trees, and the sounds of cicadas at twilight, replaced instead with Jack In The Box restaurants, Shell stations, and blaring car horns.

Texas Road Kill

Although Preston Road is not exactly well known for its haunting, it does carry with it a reputation that some consider just as sinister for others reasons. Over the years this one length of roadway has seen so many fatalities from traffic accidents that national publications such as *Road & Track Magazine*, *USA Today*, and *CNN* have listed it one of the most treacherous portions in the country. Even State Farm Insurance, one of the largest providers of auto insurance, has openly called it the most dangerous road in America.

I decided to wait until most of the road's notorious traffic had died down before paying it a visit one evening.

Hopefully, that meant a better chance of catching a glimpse of the phantoms or even a photograph if I were lucky. Most importantly, it also meant I stood a greater chance of not becoming Texas road kill.

Earlier I staked out a one-mile section of the road between the cross streets of Spring Valley and Belt Line known for having the largest number of sightings. After parking on a side street in a residential area split in half by the roadway, I grabbed my trusty camera and headed north along Preston Road on foot. While doing research for the case, I early on decided to follow (literally), in the footsteps of Mitchel Whitington, author of *Ghosts of North Texas*, who also transversed the same parcel of roadway looking for the rumored phantoms. Even though Mitchel didn't report seeing any phantoms, he does make mention of, "something on the other side of the road. I'd like to say it was grayish and moving in the opposite direction, but it was just a peripheral sight out of the corner of my eye." (Whitington 2003, 44)

My own hopes were to see something strange as well, even if it were just out of the corner of my eye—which is probably why I never saw the car barreling down on me at that moment. With my head full of ghosts, I barely heard the yellow Mustang roaring by; hugging the curb a mere few inches from where I was standing. Diving for the protection of the sidewalk I could feel the hot wind of its passing over my legs and back. By the time I looked up, the only thing remaining was the harsh smell of the car's exhaust and a few of my best obscenities. Picking up my camera, I chided myself for being so careless and determined to give the roadway a much wider berth. After all, I was here looking for ghosts, not trying to become one.

Setting off again I kept one eye out for ghosts and one out for traffic. In recent years, drivers and pedestrians alike have witnessed strange spectacles of ghostly figures moving along the side of the road. By most accounts, the phantoms are seen around dusk, just as the last of the day's sunlight gives way to the glare of city street lamps. Many of the apparitions appear as groups of figures in early pioneer clothing, making their way north as if the cars speeding by didn't exist. Others describe the forms as something more indistinct and grayish in coloration, caught only out of the corner of the eye.

Plodding along, I thought about all of those other feet that walk this same path on their long journey. Some were hunting game, others driving noisy herds of beef, and some were on their way to a new home and a fresh start. Regardless of their purpose, it now seems that a few of those early travelers never made it to their destinations and walk the road still. Crossing a bridge as an ambulance swept by in a flash of red and white with sirens blaring, I couldn't help but wonder if it was racing to the scene of some accident up the road. Perhaps something involving a yellow Mustang?

At the end of my harrowing mile hike, I sat in the parking lot of a large white office building shaped like a giant X. I hadn't seen any phantom travelers tonight, but I did begin to think a lot about why these ghosts seemed trapped to walk the same route over and over again, and an interesting idea came to mind.

Ley Lines

In 1922, an amateur archeologist and antiquarian named Alfred Watkins published a book entitled *Early British Trackways*. In the book, Alfred theorized that based on maps from his home in Balckwardine, England, he noticed that many ancient landmarks could be connected by a series of straight lines, convincing him that he had discovered an age-old trading route. These "ley lines," as they came to be called, were thought to be invisible lines of natural energy running vertically and horizontally across the earth. In turn, humans were thought to be unconsciously drawn to these sources of power, building sacred sites and burial grounds along their course. Some theorize that many traditionally haunted sites can be found where two such lines cross, creating a nodule of super-charged energy that in a sense feeds the haunting.

It was all too difficult to say at the moment and I still had another harrowing mile to trek before I reached the safety of my car again. The sun was going down as I turned back south and retraced my footsteps. It was time to leave this dangerous road and the phantoms that walked it. Maybe something is keeping them here through the centuries; something just below the surface or perhaps the ghosts that walk this path are just trying to make it home. Sometimes that's the longest trip we make.

The haunted section of Preston Road
runs north of Dallas's downtown district
bordered by the cross streets
of Spring Valley and Belt Line roads.

Lady of the Lake

*I do believe there is a practical lesson to this story,
and that is, "DON'T PICK UP HITCHHIKERS!"*
—Anonymous witness to the phantom of the lake

Late one cold and wet Halloween night after all the trick or treaters were asleep in their beds and dreaming of the candy they'd collected that night, Guy Malloy was just leaving work. As director of window displays for the Neimann-Marcus department store, his day had been both long and demanding. Rubbing the weariness from his eyes with one hand, he turned his two-door sedan onto Lawther Road, a barren track that circled the winding shores of White Rock Lake. A light drizzle began to fall and mix with the mist from the lake's waters.

Visibility was poor, and as the beams of the headlights cut through the shrouded night, a figure in white stumbled onto the road from the water's edge. Slamming the brake peddle to the floor, Guy's car slid to a halt a mere foot from where the figure stood. He could barely believe his eyes. Illuminated in the headlight's glow stood a beautiful young woman in a silken white evening gown.

Guy immediately exited the car and rushed over to the woman to make sure she was unharmed. Placing his coat around her shoulders, he ushered her into the warmth of the waiting car and noticed for the first time how deathly cold her skin felt under his hand. Other then appearing drenched to the bone and in a semi state of shock, Guy was relieved to find that she suffered no obvious injuries.

Falling harder, the drizzle soon became a downpour and as Guy Malloy pulled off again into the night, he began to feel like he had entered a terrible dream. His new passenger spoke very little other than to request that he take her home to an address she gave on nearby Gaston Avenue, an affluent neighborhood bordering lake. When pressed with further questions, she admitted to attending a formal dance that evening with her boyfriend. As the night wore on, the two began quarreling and she'd left the dance hall alone and on foot just as the rains came. Now all she wanted to do was get home before her father began to worry.

The two said very little to one another after that, as Guy concentrated on maneuvering the narrow roads along the lake until he reached the address at Gaston Avenue. Coming to a stop in the drive, he turned to his companion to ask if she needed help to the door, but to his shock he found that the mysterious woman had vanished. The only things remaining in the seat next to him were the coat he placed over her shoulders and a small puddle of water.

Bewildered by her sudden disappearance, he opened the car door and ran through the sheets of rain to the protection of the home's covered porch. The darkened house stood quietly hunched against the rain as he knocked on the front door. Thinking better of the idea, he was about to turn and leave when the door opened and an older man stepped out.

Before he could stop himself, the whole story came pouring out in a rush, from the time he picked up the stranded woman to her disappearance as he arrived at the house. The old man listened to the tale with sad, tired eyes as if he had heard the whole thing before. When Guy stopped to catch his breath, the man calmly informed him that, "No, he wasn't crazy." Indeed, he had brought the man's daughter home. Only she had died two years earlier in an auto accident on Lawther Road. Since that time, each year on the anniversary of her death, she appears to lone travelers along the lakeshore, begging them to take her home. Each time it's the same, and just before arriving at her destination, she disappears.

Guy Malloy stood there in stunned silence as the rain fell harder and the first of the storm's lightening filled the night sky.

The shores of White Rock Lake.

The story of Guy Malloy's encounter with the phantom lady of White Rock Lake has gone on to become one of Dallas's most enduring legends. Each year, as the story is retold in news articles, books, and campfire circles, the tale changes just a little, until what is truth and what is fiction no longer matters. Tracing the legend back to its original source is somewhat difficult because it's been around for such a long time.

A Legend Is Born

The first written account of the lady of the lake appears in the 1943 edition of the Texas Folklore Society's *Backwoods to Border*, under the title "The Ghost of White Rock." Other sources, however, insist that she's been around much longer, and that high school students at nearby Woodrow Wilson High had been circulating her story since the early 1930s.

These earlier versions run much the same as Guy Malloy's more modern ghost story, with a few more details to flesh it out and add more chills. This one begins on an excursion boat named the *Bonnie Barge*, which operated in the waters of White Rock Lake in the 1920s.

Each night the flat-bottomed boat toured the lake offering partygoers live entertainment and refreshments. One evening, a well dressed couple began to argue heatedly during the cruise. When the boat finally docked, the distraught young woman jumped into her escort's model T Ford without him and sped away.

Shaken by the fight and cloudy with the effects of alcohol, she took each twisting turn with reckless abandon. Around the intersection of Lawther and Garland Roads, she lost control of the vehicle, sending it careening into the dark, frigid waters of the lake and ending her life.

Since the accident, her spirit is said to appear to travelers late at night along the old road that circles the lake, still wearing the dripping-wet evening gown she died in. The rest of the story follows much of the same pattern. As the unsuspecting motorist stops to help, she begs to be taken home to a nearby address. Before reaching her destination, however, her figure evaporates into nothingness, usually leaving some object such as a coat or scarf behind as proof of the ghostly encounter.

According to famed American folklorist, Professor Jan Harold Brunvand, in his 1981 book, *The Vanishing Hitchhiker: American Urban Legends and Their Meanings*, the vanishing hitchhiker is a classic tale found in differing variants throughout the world. Beginning as far back as the 1800s, travelers told of phantom women who appeared on the back of their horses. Just like the more modern tales, these phantoms always vanish before reaching their destination and later prove to be the deceased daughter of some nearby wealthy landowner. Its modern equivalent gained popularity in the 1920s and 1930s, with the introduction of the automobile and continues even today.

In light of this, is then the ghost of White Rock Lake a mere invention or urban legend archetype or are there mitigating factors that separate it from other similar tales and lend it credibility? Answering this would be a daunting task and I quickly found that White Rock Lake does not give up its secrets—or its ghosts—so easily.

Hot on the Trail

White Rock Lake is located in east Dallas, bordered on the south by Garland Road and on the north by Mockingbird Lane. Today, most of the land running along the 9.5 miles of twisting shoreline is well kept parkland filled with jogging paths, wooden pavilions, and scenic overlooks. Before the lake became a Mecca for Dallas urbanites, the land was a shallow pecan-lined valley whose loamy soil was fed by the meandering course of Rock Creek.

The first humans known to inhabit this swath of land were wandering tribes of Anadarko, who hunted herds of bison that came to feed on the tall prairie grasses along the creek. With the founding of Dallas in the 1800s, the tribes that once called the land home were displaced. A few early pioneer families went on to farm the rich soil of the valley until after the American Civil War when it came to shelter settlements of freed slaves.

As the boundaries of the city pushed ever outward, finding a viable source of water to meet the needs of the expanding population became increasingly difficult. Until this time, Dallas relied primarily on the Trinity River and a few small artesian wells to do the job, but these were quickly strained to their limit. In response to the problem, the city began purchasing land in the small valley to the east to act as a reservoir. By 1910, a damn was completed; eventually filling the depression and giving birth to White Rock Lake. After three years of rising lake levels, the reservoir finally began pumping into the city's water mains, as well as providing coolant for new steam-electric plants.

It wasn't long before the city found this new body of water was suitable for other purposes also, and soon parks and other attractions were springing up all over its shores. The lake became such a lure for area residents that one anonymous reporter in 1927, dubbed it the "Peoples Playground." By the 1930s, beaches circled the lake, a popular dance pavilion appeared on the eastern shore, and on the western side a boathouse, with berths enough for thirty-six boats.

During the era of the Great Depression, the Civil Works Administration and the Works Progress Administration provided work by initiating projects to upgrade the lake's facilities. As a result, two new bridges were constructed on either side of the lake, in addition to a series of parks for public use.

As the nation launched itself into WWII, the government established a prisoner of war camp at Winfrey Point for soldiers captured in North Africa fighting under the command of Erwin Rommel's Afrika Corps. With the advent of the 1950s, however, the glorious dream of the "People's Playground," began to fade. Waves of vandalism, neglect, and boiling social tensions started to take their toll on the once-pristine waterway.

In the sweltering summer of 1952, amid fears of racial conflict, the city instituted a ban on swimming in the lake, which remains in affect to this very day. This alarming trend continued until the 1980s, when the citizens of Dallas, in conjunction with the city's Parks and Recreation Department, began the heroic effort to reclaim the lake. Since the initiative, the city has made tremendous strides in reestablishing the waters of White Rock Lake as a place for the people once again.

As I mentioned earlier, White Rock Lake is a place that holds many secrets within the murky depths of its waters, and separating the fact from the fiction would prove a daunting task. Like most urban legends, the stories associated with the spectral lady of the lake carry with them the accumulation of decades of storytelling, which true to their nature, leave little room for verifiable facts. Public records from the 1920s and 1930s, provide no clear evidence to substantiate the claims that a woman died in a car accident in the area at that time. In fact, even the identity of the young woman remains suspect. Although some believe that she lies buried somewhere behind the ancient gates of nearby Cox Cemetery, no one has yet proven which weathered tombstone bears her name.

Another obstacle to investigating the mystery lay in the shear size of the lake itself. With nighttime sightings from almost every quarter of the lake, surrounding woods, and roads, hunting the elusive spirit seemed an impossible task for any investigator. Then again, maybe that's what makes such tales the stuff of legends; they tantalize the imagination while remaining always just out of reach.

I was just about to throw my hands in the air and let the lady rest in peace when something began to bother me about the case. So, shifting back through the mountains of files I'd collected on the lake, I began to notice a new pattern emerging. Although many of the sightings carried with them the obvious hallmarks of an urban legend, there were others that pointed to a different, yet equally disturbing source.

Would the Real Lady of the Lake Please Step Forward?

Over the years, a number of deaths have occurred in and around the lake ranging from boating mishaps and accidental drownings to tragic suicides and murders. Some of the eyewitness accounts that I collected indicated that perhaps the haunting was the result of some other death that transpired near the lake rather than our famous hitchhiker.

For instance, on October 29, 1987, Dallas Herald Columnist Lorriane Iannello reported that a woman named Phyllis Thompson described an encounter with the phantom very different from the well-known traditional tale. According to Mrs. Thompson, she and her daughter Sue Ann Ashman were sitting on one of the many boat docks that jut out into the lake. It was a moonless night, and as the two women sat talking, they spied an object floating towards them. As it grew closer, the pale white mass rolled over in the water revealing the corpse of a woman with dark hollow sockets where the eyes should have been. Before either of the frightened women could move a muscle, the apparition dissolved in front of their eyes.

Another chance meeting with the lady of the lake involved a young couple parked along a romantically secluded section one night. As the two young lovers sat listening to the radio and gazing up at the stars (making out is probably closer to the truth), an iridescent form appeared over the water's surface some distance away. As the figure slowly approached their vehicle, it changed into the glowing, white form of a woman with her arms outstretched as if reaching for them. Shaking off his terror at the last moment, the young man slammed the car into drive and raced off, just as the apparition reached for the handle of the car door.

Even local law enforcement has revealed their share of run-ins with the phantom while patrolling the area. Charley Eckhardt, a former Dallas law officer remembers a story told to him by his long-time partner, Steve Wester, about his own experience with the ghost. During the graveyard shift one night in the mid 1960s, Officer Wester was patrolling a marshy patch of ground near the north end of the lake where Lawther Road intersects with Northwest Highway. Working his powerful spotlight at the water's edge, he spotted a woman walking out of the reeds soaking wet. Leaving the patrol car, he made his way through the swampy mire to see if she needed assistance, but as he waded closer, she simply disappeared. It would be an encounter he would never forget in all his years in law enforcement.

In spite of the fact that legend normally places the phantom along Lawther Road, I also found reports of something haunting the houses that border the lake on Garland Road. In many of these accounts the phantom is often mistaken for a living person—that is until she vanishes in front of the startled homeowner.

In 1962, a man named Dale Berry claimed that the famous phantom of the lake had dropped by for a visit one evening. It began when his doorbell rang unexpectedly. It was rather late for visitors he thought, but when he answered the door, no one was there. With a shrug of his shoulders, he returned to the television program he was watching only to have the bell ring again. And again, when he answered, the front porch was empty. Finally, the third time the bell sounded, he rushed to the door intent on nabbing the prankster. What he found instead would send him reeling.

Flinging the door open wide, Dale Berry stood face to face, not with some teenager bent on mischief, but with the apparition of a young women, her mouth open as if locked in a silent scream. Stepping back in shock, the apparition faded in front of him leaving a small pool of water on his doorstep.

In light of so many stories over the decades, it's difficult to say what exactly is haunting White Rock Lake. Is it the lure of a good ghost story passed from generation to generation or could it stem from one of the many others tragedies that have occurred in these waters? Does something wander the banks and roadways of the lake at night seeking help it will never find?

Over the years, especially around Halloween, curiosity seekers drive the roads of White Rock Lake Park hoping to catch a glimpse of the spectral lady. This has led to some frightening experiences for some, as well as some comical situations for others. In the 1940s, Dallas police were flooded with frantic calls one night from motorists driving down Lawther Road, who reported a glowing woman in white standing in the middle of the road with her arms outstretched. Squad cars were dispatched quickly and in no time the police had cracked the case. Seems that at one point along the lake road, there stood an old road sign shaped like a cross. As vehicles turned the corner their headlights illuminated the sign creating what appeared in the dark as the glowing image of a ghost.

If you're bound and determined to see the lady of the lake for yourself, then this is what I suggest you do. Wait until the moon has risen high in the night sky and the mists swirl above the lake's surface in strange patterns. Then hop in your car and travel down Lawther Road, paying attention as you go to the movement of the wind through the scattered trees and the sound of waves lapping against the lakeshore. However, if you do happen to pass some beautiful young woman in 1920s attire, think twice about stopping. Otherwise you might just be giving the famous lady of the lake a ride home that night.

White Rock Lake
located in northeast Dallas
between Garland Road and Mockingbird Lane
Web: www.whiterocklakefoundation.org

Lights on the Hill

The Summit of Flagpole Hill.

...he saw a red light before him,
as when the felled trunks and branches
of a clearing have been set on fire,
and throw up their lurid blaze against the sky,
at the hour of midnight.
He paused, in a lull of the tempest
that had driven him onward,
and heard the swell of what seemed a hymn,
rolling solemnly from a distance
with the weight of many voices.

—Nathaniel Hawthorne,
"Young Goodman Brown"

F lagpole Hill towers above the heavily-forested
landscape of White Rock Lake's northern border
like a lone sentinel standing on the horizon. As one

of the highest points in Dallas County's relatively flat geography, it's a feature that can be seen from miles in any direction. In 1936, the city of Dallas realized the picturesque value of what was then called "Doran's Point" and used the Civilian Conservation Corps to construct a scenic overlook on the crest of the hill. A huge American flag was added (hence the name Flagpole Hill) and the site became a popular place for parties, picnics, family reunions, and other public events.

Yet despite the wonder of its natural beauty, Flagpole Hill is a place haunted by tales ranging from accounts of ghastly satanic rituals to dramatic UFO sightings. Having recently wrapped up an investigation of the infamous phantom of White Rock Lake, I decided it was time to pay the nearby hill a visit and see for myself what all the fuss was about.

Strange Lights and Raining Rocks

Weaving my way through the eastbound traffic of Dallas's Northwest Highway, I watched as the bare flanks of the hill rose slowly in the distance. It was on this very road one cold, autumn night that a strange spectacle played itself out over the hill. As one eyewitness to the event later revealed, she was traveling home from work around 7 pm on November 21, 2005, when a series of bright lights suddenly appeared in the sky, bathing the hill in artificial colors.

Captivated by the drama, she watched as a large circular object with red and white lights at its perimeter came into view. While the amazing light show gripped her attention, two swift military jet fighters streaked onto the scene and maneuvered to approach the unidentified flying object from either direction. Before they could draw near, however, the alien craft rocketed up into the night sky until it disappeared from view altogether, leaving only the angry roar of jet fighters buzzing about like agitated hornets as proof of the encounter.

Zipping past the blur of neighborhoods that comprise the eastern section of Dallas, I was surprised at how quickly the cityscape gave way to the cottonwood, black willow, and hackberry that signal the beginning of White Rock Lake Park. Accelerating forward, I crossed the sluggish green waters of White Rock Creek, with its jumbled slabs of white, chalk-lined banks for which it takes its name. At the exit for Goforth Road, I left the highway turning north towards Flagpole Hill. The sun was sinking to the west and as the rising flanks of the hill grew closer, I began to get the creeping sensation that it sat hunched as if waiting for me. After approximately 150 yards, a small one-lane road, bound with cedar trees known as Doran Circle, curved its way to the top in a horseshoe shape.

Even before reports of extraterrestrial activity, Flagpole Hill carried with it a well-known reputation for the paranormal. Late at night, near the drawing of the witching hour, curious lights were said to be seen flickering on the hilltop. For those foolhardy enough to make their way up the winding roadway to investigate, another phenomenon awaited them.

Since 1976, local law enforcement have responded to calls from motorists whose cars have been inundated by sudden showers of fist-sized stones falling from the sky. These bizarre showers often cause considerable damage to the vehicles and are seen not only falling from completely clear skies, but also from angles seemingly impossible to duplicate. To this day, police have no leads to explain the activity and have yet to apprehend anyone in connection with the vandalism. However, where the paper trail of police reports end, local legend continues and stories of rock-throwing ghosts have persisted since the 1930s, when the roadbed first cut its way up the hill.

Mysterious showers of stones are nothing new in the realm of the supernatural and have been reported for centuries from just about ever corner of the world. One of the earliest examinations of the phenomenon can be traced back to the Gaelic scholar Robert Kirk, who in

Doran Circle where strange stone showers are reported.

1690, attributed reports of stone showers to subterranean inhabitants he called "invisible wights."

In our own country, the first mention of raining stones appeared in a 1698 pamphlet entitled "Lithobolia, or the Stone-throwing Devil," by Richard Chamberlain, secretary of the colony of New Hampshire.

The most famous case of falling stones, however, has to go to the Bell Witch haunting in 1817. In addition to other strange going-ons during the haunting, witnesses testified that stones were thrown at Bell family members by an unseen entity, conjured up by a local witch.

Keeping in mind the road's reputation, I flipped on my headlights and nervously made the ascent as the shadows along the way lengthened in the coming dusk. Admittedly, once I reached the top I breathed a gentle sigh of relief and relaxed my grip on the steering wheel—after all, I don't think my car insurance covers supernatural showers of stones.

Disappearing Islands and Dark Rituals

Parking my car on the road's narrow shoulder, I watched the last of the sun's rays wash orange and red over the hill's western slope. A short distance to the south lay the darkening waters of White Rock Lake and the origin of one of the area's more light-hearted tales. Long time residents here say that if you stand atop Flagpole Hill at twilight and gaze out across the surface of the lake, an island will appear as if floating on the water.

Known as the magical island of Bonnie Belle, the truth behind the legend stems from a recurring error by cartographers while drawing maps of the lake. For some reason they kept drawing in a bit of land where none existed. In time, the "phantom island" grew until its story fused with the local lore of the lake, drawing curiosity seekers to the hill at sundown hoping to catch a glimpse of it.

Unfortunately, I, like so many others before me, would come to find no such fabled isle dancing on the distant waters. What

I did find was a breath-taking expanse of forest, carpeting the land between the hill and the lakeshore as a solitary egret took flight over the calm waters just before night settled in.

There was one last task to perform before leaving Flagpole Hill, and with the trusty flashlight that I'm almost never without these days, I began to scour the ground around me. Of the hill's more sinister associations is the claim that horrid satanic rituals take place here on moonless nights. In fact, some whisper that it's the devilish flames of their sacrificial fires burning through the night that accounts for the strange lights above the hill.

What I was looking for was the telltale signs of occult activity that might add some validity to the rumors of devil-worshippers. Instead of used fire pits, discarded black candles, and satanic glyphs carved in the ground, I found empty beer bottles, spent cigarettes, and a raccoon trying to get into a garbage can. Not quiet the nefarious evidence I had hoped for.

It was late when I finally turned back onto the busy highway for the far-off comfort of home. To be honest, I was a little disappointed in the outcome. There were no great showers of rocks pummeling my car, no evil Satanists to run from, no enchanted isle in the distance, and certainly no little green men with an itch to probe things; then again maybe it was a good thing I didn't run into any of these.

With Flagpole Hill retreating in the distance, I thought about looking back in my rearview mirror and seeing if perhaps the hill was bathed in strange dancing spirit lights, but then I thought better of it. I think I'll leave this one to my imagination…and yours.

Flagpole Hill
Flagpole Hill Park
8700 East Northwest Highway
Dallas, Texas 75238

A Night in a Haunted House

For over all there hung a cloud of fear.
A sense of mystery the spirit daunted,
And said as plain as a whisper in the ear,
"The place is haunted."

—Thomas Hood, "The Haunted House"

S ometimes the greatest adventures in life find their beginnings in places you would never imagine. One minute you're entertaining guests at a dinner party over a few bottles of wine, and the next thing you know, you're locked in a haunted house alone all night. Perhaps I'm getting a little ahead of myself.

It all started during a round of ghost stories one night with a few of my friends. As is often my custom after too much wine, I love regaling anyone who will listen to a few of the juiciest stories I've culled from investigations over the years. Just as I finished the most ghastly tale I thought I could muster, a friend named Kenneth Sutherland spoke up after a polite pause and interjected a ghost story of his own.

It surprised me to say the least; Kenneth was a talented and successful artist, but a teller of ghost stories was something new for him. Pretty soon, however, I too was listening with rapt attention, just like the other partygoers.

For generations along his wife's line, Kenneth's family owned a sprawling mansion in one of Dallas's more affluent suburbs along Forest Lane. Although the property has since passed to the Unity Church of Dallas, which the family regularly attends, the Sutherlands maintained a close eye on their ancestral property. Since the property was transferred, it has become known as the "White House," and routinely plays host to wedding receptions and other formal events.

In time, the house began to develop a reputation for more than just lavish balls and receptions. Soon, stories were spreading from nervous employees and startled guests that spirits of the dead walked its empty rooms. Encounters with a floating woman in white, bone-chilling cold spots, and phantom music added to the mysterious legends of the home. Some of the staff were at their wits end and no one wanted to be alone in the house at night. When Kenneth finished his intriguing tale, a devilish grin spread across his face.

"Well, how about it?" he looked at me.

"How 'bout what?"

"Care to spend the night? By yourself, of course."

That's how it all started, a simple challenge over a round of ghost stories. I heartily agreed to the proposal and Kenneth promised to make the necessary arrangements the following day. As the hour grew late and the last of the guests departed, the courage-enhancing effects of the wine began to wear off and I started to wonder—what in the world did I just get myself into?

History of the Haunting

Several days later, true to his word, Kenneth introduced me to Pat McBride, Event Coordinator for the "White House." A charming woman with a real fascination for ghosts, Pat knew more about the property than anyone else alive and was certainly happy to fill in the details for me. According to her, construction on the home began in 1941, and finished sometime in 1947. The house was designed in the Greek Revival Colonial style popular in southern plantation homes before the American Civil War. Symmetrically shaped with bold yet simple moldings and a columned entry, the structure closely resembled something from a backdrop of *Gone with the Wind*. In fact, the "White House" is thought to be one of the purist forms of such architecture remaining in the south today.

The Dallas White House.

Historical records show that the "White House" was built by R. B. Evans, Jr., for his wife Susannah and was molded after his boyhood home in Vicksburg, Mississippi. R. B. it seems was having an extremely difficult time convincing his wife that the family should move to Texas. Susannah was dead set against the matter and contrived what she thought would be a sure-fire way to avoid it. Of course she would relocate, but on one condition; he would have to build an exact replica of his boyhood home in Mississippi. This was a task she was sure would be impossible for anyone, even her hardworking husband. Imagine her surprise when R. B. actually pulled it off and she was forced to move after all.

It was no easy task mind you, given the cost of building material during WWII, and R. B. was forced to scavenge the necessary supplies from a number of sources. Three thousand stone blocks, some weighing as much as thirty-five pounds apiece, were taken from the old Dallas post office for its construction. In addition, 42,000 bricks of Trinity River clay, 5,000 square feet of Beechwood flooring from an abandoned factory, and 12 gigantic columns from a nearby mansion rounded out the job. As a finishing touch, R. B. had heavy Italian "milk marble" shipped from his boyhood home to be used for mantel pieces in the building's numerous fireplaces. Rare even then, "milk marble" is unattainable today.

Although no one is known to have died in the home, Pat McBride was quick to point out that many believe the ghost haunting the premises is none other than Susannah Evans come back to find out what all the ruckus is about.

One story Pat shared with me involved an account by the facility manager who felt a strong presence following him through the house as he made his rounds one day. Climbing the grand staircase to the second floor, he began to hear the sounds of piano keys being struck, slowly and randomly, in a room off to his right.

Determined to investigate the sounds, he entered the bare room just as the music stopped. To his knowledge there never was a piano in the house during the time that he worked there.

On another occasion, while installing a new doorbell, the manager shut the front door from the outside and was just about to ring the bell when he heard the sounds of muffled conversation coming from inside. Placing his ear to the door's surface, the noise sounded garbled and indistinguishable, but when he yanked the door open, the empty foyer was quiet again.

Others have had their share of run-ins with the house's spirits as well. One staff member was locking the house up for the night when he received the scare of his life. Having checked the house thoroughly he set the building's alarm code and moved towards his car waiting in the parking lot. A movement caught his eye and looking back at the house he noticed a set of double doors on the second floor standing wide open. Swearing he had latched them tight while closing up, he entered the house again and secured them a second time. Thinking all was well, he was just about to climb into his car, when he looked back again only to discover the same set of double doors standing open. This time however, he felt it more prudent to come back in the morning and check things over. Ghost or no ghost, something wanted those doors left open and he was just fine with that.

In time it wasn't long before visitors to the house were reporting strange tales of their own. One evening, a group of women were leaving the house after a reception. The event went longer than anyone expected, and by the time they reached their cars, night had already fallen. While saying their goodbyes to one another, several of the women looked up to the house and gasped in unison. There in a second-story window facing the small group stood the headless torso of a woman in a glowing white dress. No one could believe their eyes, as the phantom stood motionless before fading into the heavier darkness of the house's window.

There were more stories to be sure, toilets flushing by themselves, objects hurtling towards unexpected victims, doors opening and shutting of their own accord, and numerous sounds that couldn't be explained. Having gathered as many of these stories as I possibly could from the helpful Mrs. McBride, we made arrangements to meet at the "White House" shortly before dark.

It Begins

When I arrived at the park-like grounds that make up the property, I was struck by a sense of being transported back in time. The house itself sits on a slight rise overlooking well-spaced oaks sagging with the heaviness of time. I almost expected to hear the clatter of carriage wheels driving up the lane or the melodies of workers singing in the fields. Instead, the traffic noise from nearby streets assaulted me, reminding me that just outside these lush grounds, a residential neighborhood had sprung up around it.

Inside the mansion, marble fireplaces dominated rooms filled with hardwood floors and soaring ceilings. An exquisitely crafted staircase marched from the foyer to the upper levels, which were cluttered with various office furniture and moldering boxes.

My first task was to meet with Gary Hoffmeier, a sensitive who has visited the house many times in the past and witnessed several phantoms first hand. We toured the place together going from each room recording his impressions. Disappointingly, he wasn't able to sense anything at that time, but he did recount his experiences from the past.

The first spirit he encountered in the house occurred one night after a wedding reception. He happened to walk into the dining room of the west wing by himself when he was struck by the image of a woman with a slight build and pointy nose. The apparition lasted but a moment, then faded into nothingness.

The second apparition was much stronger in both imagery and what Gary called "intent." This one he witnessed standing outside the house near the rear entrance. It was a man dressed in shabby work clothes, with a stern, weathered look about him. He also gave off an air of discomfort, as if he knew he didn't belong there. As we were wrapping the show up, Pat McBride entered and handed me a key to the front door.

Voices in the Dark

"Now here dear," she said sweetly, offering me the key. "And here's my number in case…well in case you run into any problems."

Despite her ominous send off, I was eager to get everyone out of the house and begin setting up. Locking myself in, I set immediately to work, and believe me, there was a lot to do.

I first made sure the building was sealed up tight with motion detectors on both doors to discourage intrusion. Then I drew up a rough floor plan making note of electrical outlets and appliances that might interfere with the equipment I'd brought or give false positives. When finished, I killed the power to the house and flooded it with darkness.

Night had come and the moon was high in the sky, casting strange shadows through the windows. The place was full of odd sounds that an overactive imagination could do wonders with. From creaking floorboards to scurrying sounds in the attic, the house had a life of its own.

Interestingly enough, I found that the Beechwood floors running through all three levels of the house acted as an immense conductor for vibrations and noises. Stomp your foot at one end of the house and the muffled tread of ghostly footsteps sounded at the other end, two floors down. I also discovered what I thought might be the source of the mysterious cold spots said to range throughout the house.

Interior of the Dallas White House.

Pouring baby powder into the vents of the antiquated duct system, I followed the powdery currents throughout the rooms and found that they lay directly in the path of known cold spots. From that it was easy to imagine a cool draft becoming proof of spiritual activity to someone familiar with the stories surrounding the house.

As the night wore on, I made my rounds checking cameras and microphones. Each report of paranormal activity I found had an easy explanation. The doors being solid wood were heavy and off center, so they had a tendency to open and shut by themselves and the latches that secured most of the windows were worn and in need of repair. The "White House" was quickly turning from a house of horror to a place that just needed a few improvements.

About 4 am, I decided to walk the grounds in hopes of picking up some activity outside the house if not in. Rounding one corner, I shined my flashlight up into the windows of the second-story and stopped cold in my tracks. There, in the window above stood the headless apparition of a woman in a long white dress.

Immediately I raced back into the house not knowing what I would do if I did come face to face with the legendary phantom. Sometimes you forget to think about such things when you need to the most. Tripping the motion detectors, I flew up the staircase; the entire house filling with the sounds of alarms. Bursting into the room, I came to a screeching halt. There was my headless phantom all right—a stuffed antique dress torso like the one's used by dress makers propped against the window. The moonlight illuminated its distorted figure in ghostly colors as it streamed through the glass.

A part of me was relieved that I hadn't run into something I couldn't handle, while another part was disappointed that I had solved so many of the house's stories. The house was alive and inviting when it had an air of mystery, but stripped of that it was nothing more than board and brick.

The sun would be up soon, so I decided to begin the lengthy pack up process. When the car was loaded I hit the road. I had survived a night in the "White House" and lived to tell the tale. Driving down the highway I popped in one of the audio recordings from the servants' quarters on the third floor. I thought I might as well get a head start on the hours and hours of tape there was to listen to.

The tape began playing the expected backgrounds noises you'd come to find in an old house. A creak here, a pop there, but then something unexpected sounded on the tape, as I slammed on the brakes and pulled the car over to the shoulder of the highway. Again and again I listened to the tape as early morning traffic sped by. I couldn't believe my ears. A low raspy male voice sounded as clear as day. It said:

Help me.

The Dallas "White House"
6525 Forest Lane
Dallas, Texas 75230
Phone: 972.991.9333
Web: www.unitydallas.org

The Ghost Hunter and the Graveyard

The Gates of Baccus Cemetery.

Remember friends as you pass by,
As you are now so once was I;
As I am now so you must be.
Prepare for death and follow me.

—Inscription on a grave marker
in Baccus Cemetery

The old, gray Chevrolet roared through the cold, October night like a phantom in the moonlight as it moved eastbound on Headquarters Drive. Inside, a young man drummed his fingers against the steering wheel as he hurried home from his part-time job at the local pizzeria. Turning the radio's volume up a little more, he angled the vehicle south onto Bishop Road and away from the nearby lights of Dallas.

Although Bishop Road was a lonely stretch of pavement running right by Baccus Cemetery, the young man knew it was a shortcut that promised to save time. He'd heard stories from his friends at school about the place—how the ghost of a man walks the cemetery at night waiting for travelers to break down on the road next to the cemetery.

For a moment, the thought of coming so close to the cemetery didn't seem like such a good idea after all, and he considered turning around to avoid the accursed spot, but it was already too late.

Traveling past the open fields that fill the area, an iron fence began to run parallel to the road's shoulder marking the eastern boundary of the creepy grounds. Suddenly a flash erupted from the passing graveyard, illuminating the landscape in an eerie glow. More bursts of light follow, silhouetting strange misshapen figures moving through the tombstones. Pressing his foot to the accelerator, the old Chevrolet rocketed forward, leaving the last of the haunted cemetery with its strange lights and silent specters behind.

As the Chevrolet retreated into the night, kicking up clouds of dust from the road, the figure of a man stepped from behind a grave marker. Removing the duel tube night-vision goggles from his face he waved a small handheld EMF meter in front of him. With each high-pitch squawk of the device, he squinted at the changing numbers on the instrument's illuminated dial. Extracting a digital camera from the pocket of his field vest he depressed the trigger, snapping yet another photograph. The cemetery brightened in the artificial glare of the flash, momentarily casting the cemetery grounds in weird shapes. Examining the recently taken photograph on the camera's LCD screen, a frown spread across his face in the darkness.

"Way too much dust," he muttered, and placing the night vision goggles on once again, he turned to move deeper into the burial grounds, until he was swallowed by the darkness of the night.

Although the young man might be thinking that he nearly escaped the dreaded clutches of the infamous phantom and no doubt will repeat the harrowing tale tomorrow at school, he had no idea that what he did glimpse was something equally unique. What he actually saw that night among the old, weathered markers was a Baccus Cemetery ghost hunter.

A Ghost Hunter's Playground

Baccus Cemetery has always attracted ghost hunters with the promise of a spook or two, and for those stalking its nocturnal grounds, it rarely disappoints. Claims of paranormal activity within its boundaries have persisted for years, attesting to a wide range of unexplained phenomena. Many reports from eyewitnesses include encounters with cold spots, photographs of orbs, phantom footsteps, disembodied voices, and apparitional forms seen out of the corner of the eye.

In addition to the good old-fashioned ghost hunting that goes on here, some groups use it as a sort of supernatural training ground, where they can hone their investigative skills and test newly purchased equipment. In fact, given the popularity of the place and its easy accessibility to the public, this once-quiet country cemetery has now become something of a ghost hunters' playground.

Located at the northwest corner of Bishop Road and Legacy Drive in Plano; Baccus Cemetery looks like the last place you might think to find restless spirits or prowling ghost hunters. Resting atop bare fields of stubby grass, it offers little more than a few scattered trees and a fence line that ends at a simple gate with the words "Baccus" above it. In the distance, rise the massive corporate office buildings and intersecting highways that have become a signature of north Dallas, replacing what was once open land stretching as far as the eye could see.

Hallowed History

When immigrants first arrived in their ox-drawn wagons from north of the Red River, they found the local population of Comanche Indians less than enthusiastic to see them. As a result, two of the first families to settle the land, McBain Jameson and Jeremiah Muncey, were massacred in 1844. Undeterred by the hostile reception, settlers continued to pour in from places as far away as Tennessee and Kentucky, through incentives of cheap land offered by the Peter's Colony Enterprise.

Unable to stem the tide, local tribes settled on a new tactic, "If you cannot live with 'em, well then, just move away," and so packing up their teepees and loading their dog-drawn travois, they left for good.

After the Comanche's departure and with the land firmly in their possession, the settlers established a town they called Plano, which meant "flat" in Spanish and reflected the surrounding terrain.

In time, the tiny hamlet developed into a thriving rural farming community until, like many small southern towns, it languished throughout the American Civil War and following Reconstruction.

In 1881, it faced another setback when a fire, which began in the basement of Kendall's Cider Saloon, engulfed the town and reduced it to ashes. Records indicate that perhaps more than fifty buildings were destroyed in the blaze, and over night, Plano became a city of tents.

In 1888, with prospects looking grim, the railroad came to town and brought the promise of new life by opening up fresh commercial markets for the community. In as little as two years time, the withering little town of Plano became a boomtown with over 1,200 souls and not one, but two important rail lines. Today, even though Plano is legally a municipality of its own, it has long given way to its larger neighbor to the south and is now considered by most a suburb of Dallas.

Baccus Cemetery was initially known as Cook Cemetery and contains one of the oldest graves in Plano. Henry Cook, a veteran of the War of 1812, was one of the first to settle the land in 1845, without losing his scalp to Indian raiders. His simple home of logs and animal hides located near the site became a landmark for travelers on the Shawnee Trail.

The first internment the property saw occurred in 1847, when Henry Cook laid his son, Daniel, to rest in its hard ground. Later Cook's daughter, Rachel Cook Baccus, donated the land for the construction of the Baccus Christian Church Sanctuary. By 1915, the now public Cook Cemetery, which held other prominent Plano families as well, was renamed Baccus Cemetery in honor of Rachel. Even though the church that once sat adjacent to the grounds was disbanded in the 1930s, the cemetery is still in use today.

Responding to the Call

In order to better understand why so many local ghost hunters have been drawn to this quiet little corner of Dallas, I decided to contact veteran paranormal researcher Chris Mosley. Besides founding the north Texas research group, Dagulf's Ghost, Chris lectures throughout the southwest on topics of the paranormal and has spent many a night investigating Baccus Cemetery.

What first peaked his interest in the case were a series of emails he received by witnesses claiming to see shadowy apparitions crossing the road between the burial ground and a nearby field. Always up for a good adventure, Chris and his team of ghost hunters responded to the call with an investigation of their own. Using many of the high tech

One of the many ancient stones that fill the cemetery.

instruments familiar to researchers in the field, including EMF meters, infrared cameras, night vision optics, and thermal gauges, Dagulf's Ghost set out to prove whether or not the site was haunted. Although Chris and his crew were skeptical about what they would uncover, their assessment of the place would change after just a few hours.

During one investigation, while filming a segment for the local channel 5 news entitled *Haunted Texas*, the team experienced the high EMF fluctuations often associated with a haunting, as well as cold spots measuring as much as a twenty degree drop in temperature. The best was yet to come however.

While experimenting with new military-grade night vision goggles on loan from the U.S. Air Force, Chris beheld a startling development unfold through the green lenses. While scanning the cemetery grounds, he watched as a white ball appeared and then dissipated into a mist-like mass. Within a matter of minutes the mass moved and shifted, taking on an almost humanoid form. Removing the goggles, he noticed the form was not visible to the naked eye, nor did the apparition appear on any of the team's other instruments.

This led Chris to a rather interesting theory about the nature of spirit orbs often seen in relation to a haunting. He believes that spirit orbs are merely a transitional phase for anomalous energy and only the beginning of a manifestation.

As the night wore on, other phenomena occurred, including one incident that happened while Chris was returning to his car to fetch another armload of equipment. Crossing the cemetery, he began to perceive the sounds of someone following closely behind him. Stopping short, he quickly turned and snapped a picture with a camera he had on hand and managed to photograph what he believes was a spirit anomaly. Apparently Chris had run into the cemetery's resident spook, and even worse, it was following him.

Although Dagulf's Ghost has moved on to other promising cases since that time, they still continue to receive the occasional email from someone claiming to have encountered the phantom of Baccus Cemetery. As of yet, no one has been able to put forth a plausible explanation as to who or what haunts these hallowed grounds, but rest assured that Baccus will continue to lure ghost hunters for some time to come.

So whether you're a seasoned professional loaded to the hilt with ghost-hunting equipment or a simple ghost enthusiast looking for a good story, Baccus Cemetery might be the place for you. If you do plan on visiting the ancient burial ground some night, take heed of the shadowy figures you see wandering through the headstones. They could just be fellow ghost hunters with the same idea, then again…

Baccus Cemetery
located at Legacy Drive and Bishop Road
just east of the North Dallas Tollway

Fright Night

The gates of Reindeer Manor.

From ghoulies and ghosties and long leggety beasties
and things that go bump in the night,
Good Lord, deliver us!

—Scottish saying

Each year during the month of October, when the nights grow longer and the air turns crisp in the autumn breeze, many of Dallas's more adventurous souls don their scariest, blood-stained costumes for a night promising both fun and fright.

Piling into cars they travel the distance to the small township of Red Oak, just south of the sprawling metropolis of Dallas off of Interstate 35. Having arrived, they carefully navigate the old rut-filled roads that wind through crowded stands of Texas Oak to where a rambling structure of red brick masonry known as Reindeer Manor awaits them. Passing through the iron gates, topped with ferocious dragons, they take their place among the other Halloween ghosts and ghouls in a line that coils its way to the very entrance of the haunted house. Inching forward one dreadful step at a time they pass Styrofoam headstones and cardboard caskets as eerie music fills the air. The tension builds until finally they stand before the gaping portal of the mansion itself.

Do they dare enter the dark building and brave the dangers that await them?

Nightmares Aplenty

Purchasing their tickets, they take a deep breath and step inside. The next half hour promises to be a nightmare unlike any they could have possibly dreamed. A hectic phantasm of running through passages shrouded in fog, where zombies, blood-covered corpses, and chainsaw-wielding madmen lurk. Sound effects scream out and strobe lights flash as each new chamber they enter holds scenes more gruesome than the next. Stumbling, almost blind at times, they make their way through medieval torture chambers, mad scientist's laboratories, and haunted crypts until finally they reach an empty room.

After being chased through the nightmarish realm of Reindeer Manor, they begin to think that perhaps they have survived everything the house could throw at them—and that's when the unthinkable happens. The door to the room suddenly closes, trapping them inside just as the ceiling slowly begins to descend on them. There's no way out, no place to run and hide, and just when they think the end is near, a small trap door opens in an opposite wall. Rushing through the escape hatch they find themselves again in the cool night air and free of the manor's deadly grip.

From behind them, the screams of those still inside can be heard and as they pause to give their racing hearts a chance to slow they smile—after all, they have just survived Reindeer Manor, one of Dallas's most popular haunted attractions. Perhaps now they'll shuffle over to the fairway for roasted corn or the ever-delightful severed head toss. Some might even chance the dangers of the manor a second or third time.

Yet regardless of terrors that await each of them, when the year passes by and autumn arrives once again, they'll be back for another shot at the manor and another night of fright.

Behind the Scenes

Reindeer Manor is currently owned by Jim Scott and operated by the Duncanville Boy Scouts. It first began its rein of terror back in 1974, but since that time, the project has taken on a life of its own with crowds swelling the fairground each season in greater numbers. In 2007, Jim Scott estimates that as many as 11, 000 people from all over the north Texas area passed through the gates of the manor.

To keep pace with the growing demand of haunted house connoisseurs, each year the attraction pushes the limits of horror, offering the latest special effects and other entertainment, including sword swallowers and fortune tellers. Yet each member of the manor's staff, from the ticket counters to the walking dead are volunteers, who each season return for nothing more than to bask in the pure enjoyment of scaring their fellow man to death. Add to this a supporting cast of off-season clean up and maintenance crews and you will find that running a project this size takes about 250 committed volunteers.

However, of all the brave souls that pass through the haunted grounds each Halloween season, few truly know the real secrets that wait behind the Manor's walls or the tragic history that has plagued its very beginning. Perhaps if they did, they might think twice before setting foot in the manor, because even among the workers that staff the attraction, there are places where they fear to go.

As this case would come to reveal, Reindeer Manor is a place where the shadows and the specters are not always tricks of special effects or rubber-masked monsters, but something far more real, and far more sinister.

In an attempt to unmask the secrets that lie here, I joined paranormal researchers from both DFW Ghost Hunters and Lone Star Paranormal on a nightlong investigation of the Manor House in what would prove to be a fright night of our very own.

It was a cold November night when we arrived shortly before midnight and began the process of unpacking the equipment we were to use. The full moon perched high in the night sky and provided us an eerie light to work by. Lifting the heavy crates of cameras and power cables from the back of the van, I looked up at the dark structure and wondered what was waiting for us inside.

Even with the glare of the moon illuminating the landscape, the Manor appeared darker than anything else around it. It was almost as if the blackness that hung about the empty windows was something that chased away the feeble light of the moon. The season had ended weeks ago, and with the crowds and staff gone for the year, the sobering thought hit us all—that we would be venturing in completely alone.

A Murderous History

The land that the manor now sits on was first owned by a man named James Sharp, a wealthy oil pioneer and banker, who built a two-story wooden house on the site and leased it to a family of Swedish immigrants to work the land. In 1915, tragedy struck the homestead when a fire that started during a lightening storm consumed the house, killing everyone inside, including several small children.

Undaunted by the loss of his poor tenants, James Sharp was quick to begin construction on a second house. This time, he would build more than a mere sharecropper's shack, but a stately manor house where he and his family could retreat to from time to time. Fearing a repeat of the tragedy that took the lives of his former tenants, James

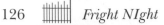

Reindeer Manor.

Sharp decided that the new home would be completely fireproof. From top to bottom, the structure was composed entirely of strong, nonflammable materials such as concrete, brick, and steel, tripling the cost of construction.

Yet if the wealthy James Sharp hoped to cheat death by building an impenetrable home of brick and steel to withstand storms or raging fires, he would soon learn that it doesn't always come from the direction you expect it to. James Sharp died in Oak Cliff, Dallas, before the completion of the manor in Red Oak.

The circumstances surrounding his death are both sketchy and suspect at best, but it is believed that he was shot in the head by a women rumored to be his mistress. Of course, more might have been revealed if Sharp's grieving widow had not used the family's considerable fortune and influence to hush the matter up as quickly as possible. The only evidence remaining from the period is a suspicious autopsy report from the coroner's office that simply reads that James Sharp died from "the loss of 2-3 ounces of brain substance."

In 1917, James Sharp, Jr., moved into the newly completed Manor House with his family. Like his father before him, James Jr., had a natural flare for making money and developed prosperous farming, ranching, and horse breeding operations on the property. Business was good, and between 1918 and 1928, the Manor grew to include additional structures such as servants' quarters, a carriage house, and a large brick barn.

With the Great Depression of 1929, however, James Jr., would watch his fortune suddenly take a turn for the worse, and the tiny empire James Jr. had laboriously created began to crumble. His wife nonetheless, refused to believe that the family's misfortune was linked to the economic recession gripping the country, but rather began to believe that the family was the victim of a curse. In the meantime, under ever increasing financial pressures, James Jr. began a steady withdraw from the public and rarely left the safety of the manor, giving rise to rumors of insanity.

Other stories began to circulate that James Jr. and his wife were spending more and more time in what the manor servants came to call "unholy pursuits." Mrs. Sharp had dabbled spiritualism for years and now began to hold nightly séances to find a solution to the family's financial problems. It is unsure just what occurred during those dark séances, but one day the manor servants arrived to find Mrs. Sharp dead in the main dining room. It appeared that she had been poisoned.

A frantic search of the property ensued until the body of James Jr. was found as well—swinging from the rafters of the barn by a noose. To this day, the deaths of Mr. and Mrs. Sharp remain a puzzling mystery and it is uncertain if the act was the result of a murder-suicide or if each chose to end their lives in a suicide pact.

For many long years, the old manor sat empty and probably would have weathered away in the harsh Texas elements if it had not been built to withstand all that nature could possibly throw at it. Of course, various owners came and went, each trying to make a go of the place, and in turn, each failed for one reason or another. The manor's once well-kept lanes became choked with undergrowth and rumors began to spring up among the nearby townsfolk of Red Oak that the land was cursed. The property was shunned by most passersby—that is until it became a haunted attraction.

Back to Business

Now with the morbid history of the place ever present in our minds, we began a planning session on the Manor's front lawn and decided to separate into teams of two or three before entering the building. This not only allowed us to cover a larger area more effectively, but also made negotiating the cramped, maze-like corridors of the manor much easier.

Each team it was decided would consist of a cameraperson and one or two others monitoring scanning equipment, such as electromagnetic field meters (EMF) or thermometers. If paranormal activity did register on the monitoring equipment during the team's sweep, the cameraperson could then be directed as to where and when to begin photographing.

After being assigned to a team of my own, we quickly split away from the main body and entered the blackness of the manor. There would be no power in the house that night and the few small headlamps worn by the others did little to pierce the almost stygian gloom. As we made our way through the convoluted passages filled with plastic skeletons, fake spider webs, and mechanical monsters, it was clear that getting lost in the macabre maze was an easy option.

Even switching to the infrared night visions goggles loaned to us for the investigation did little to help. Instead, it simply made the attraction's gruesome displays that much more disturbing in its resulting green picture. Under these conditions, it was easy to see how the mind could begin playing tricks on a person. Even the simplest noises echoed oddly within the manor and the air hung heavy and damp until breathing in the confined corridors became difficult.

About midway through the manor, the hallway opened to reveal a scene taken straight from Bram Stoker's *Dracula*. We had entered a crypt of sorts, complete with an old pipe organ and a coffin designed to spring open and scare unwary visitors. This was as creepy a place as any to take a break and so we rested a few moments to recalibrate out instruments and collect ourselves.

It also gave me time to review some of the paranormal activity that has been reported in the manor over the years. Richard Kinney, the Public Relations Chairman for Reindeer Manor, was kind enough to fill me in on the strange events that were spooking the volunteers who worked here. Some of the workers believed that their experiences were the result of an over-active imagination, while others were sure that what they encountered in the dark manor was the work of actual spirits. The one thing that both had in common was the fact that at the end of the season, each walked away with a disturbing tale or two of their own.

Tales to Tell

One such tale common among the staff involved reports by volunteers that, while working in the Manor, they sometimes feel as if they are being followed around by an unseen presence. Often, the distinct sound of footsteps can be heard creeping along just behind them, yet when they turn to confront the noise, no one is there and the phantom footsteps have stopped.

Another auditory manifestation that has given more than one staff member a shock includes the sound of a woman moaning in the former dining room where the poisoned body of Mrs. Sharp was found long ago. Those brave enough to investigate the sound say that it always fades away just as they enter the room, and regardless of how hard they search, no source or explanation can be found.

However, of all the stories told about the manor's ghostly happenings, the strangest seems to center around the building's attic. Now used as a storage space and dressing room for the volunteers, the attic is a jumble of old boxes splitting apart, moth-eaten costumes, and dark, drafty corners. It's here that while preparing for a night of spooking, workers claim the room will suddenly grow cold as they feel the overwhelming sensation that someone or something is standing right next to them.

Oddly enough, the presence always seems to be to the right of them and some say they have even felt an invisible hand come to rest on their shoulders or backs. At other times, members of the staff recount hearing a voice call out in the attic, which they describe as a long soft whisper that, before it fades out of hearing, sounds like a man saying "are you here to…" or "have you come to…."

Of those who have encountered the phantom of the attic, few wish to return, and even fewer do so alone or at night. It's fun to scare people they say, but not many of the volunteers appreciate being on the receiving end of it.

Another paranormal hot spot on the Manor's grounds can be located in the old stone barn that once witnessed the end of James Jr. by means of a hangman's noose. Since the manor became a commercial haunted house, the barn has been converted into what is now known as the 13th Street Morgue and functions as a smaller, yet equally scary, attraction. Here too sightings abound of supernatural activity, including reports of what is described as a "shadow person" moving about the building. For those who have seen the dark entity themselves, they state that it is as if a shadow is being cast by a man, yet there is no one there to cast it.

Crescendo

Back at the manor, the team was up and moving again as we made our way through the remainder of the building. Little had occurred during our sweep, other than a few scares from fake cobwebs in the face or occasionally running into some mechanical monster we weren't expecting. Yet we still had one last place to investigate, and as we ascended the creaky wooden staircase to the attic, none of us could foresee what was about to happen.

Earlier in the evening other teams radioed in that foot steps were heard thumping around in the attic while no one was there. Although the attic was now quiet, we eagerly began setting up audio equipment in the hope of catching a disembodied voice or two on tape.

Normally the process of capturing the sounds of a spirit, known as electronic voice phenomena (EVP), begins with researchers asking aloud a series of questions in order to prompt the spirit to respond in some way. These can be as simple as asking the spirit what its name is or as challenging as demanding it show some sign of its presence; all the while of course the recorders are rolling to capture the event. With the cameras and other equipment now in place the team gathered around the recorder to initiate the EVP session.

Carl Hullett, veteran ghost hunter and member of DFW Ghost Hunters, began by first depressing the record button and then logging in the time, date, and location for future reference. After a few simple questions to get the ball rolling we moved on to more direct inquires like the always nervous "give us a sign that you exist" kind of stuff.

The room unexpectedly became colder at that point and the hair on our arms stood on end. Before any of us could react, we watched in amazement as the stop button on the audio recorder depressed by itself—as if someone was stopping the tape. This unusual action was then followed by the rewind button, then the stop button again, and finally the play button. It was as if some invisible force had stopped the recording, hit the rewind button, stopped it again, and then hit play right before our very eyes. It appears that we were given exactly what we had asked for.

Time slipped by in the dark attic space, and although the temperature of the air returned to normal, there still remained a sharp electrical quality to it. As our initial excitement started to wear off, we mulled over numerous possibilities to explain the recorder's curious behavior. Our investigation was drawing to a close and we rounded up our equipment and headed back to the Manor's front lawn to take a head count. We knew we were leaving the darkness of the building behind us.

We had come that night hoping to find something within the bizarre walls of Reindeer Manor and in truth we did. Why the recorder acted as strangely as it did is hard to explain without pondering a supernatural answer, but it was witnessed by several researchers.

Following the investigation, I would find myself drawn back to the Manor several times for interviews,

Looking down from where James Jr. hung himself in the barn.

photographs, and further investigations, and each time I entered the place, it was as if the house itself were watching my every move. Reindeer Manor has certainly seen its share of the extraordinary and the grotesque over the years. Numerous violent deaths have occurred there, as well as attempts by the Sharp family to open a portal to the spirit world in their drive to answer the problems that were plaguing them. Who knows then what they invited into that house with their dark dabbling, or is it they who still wander the lonely manor halls at night?

Reindeer Manor is a wonderful place to visit if you want the socks scared off of you. Just remember when you enter through its dark doors, that maybe, just maybe, not all the ghosts and ghouls that inhabit it are made of rubber and fake blood. Some just might be the real thing. So when you run through the Manor, chased by some horrid monster, run fast, and when you scream, scream loud.

Reindeer Manor
410 Houston School Road
Red Oak, Texas 75154
Phone: 972-218-RATS
Web: www.reindeermanor.com

For further information on this popular haunted attraction please see the "More Boo for the Buck" section of this book.

Mystery of the Wax Museum

To you they are wax,
but to me their creator,
they live and breathe.

—Vincent Price,
"House of Wax"

I n 1953, audiences sat glued to the edge of their theater
seats as the master of horror, Vincent Price, lurked
across the screen while sinister music filled the air in
the movie *House of Wax*. Based largely on the earlier 1933
version entitled, *Mystery of the Wax Museum,* Price plays
the role of crazed wax sculptor, Professor Henry Jarrod.
After a fire set by his less than scrupulous business partner
leaves him horribly disfigured and unable to use his hands
for sculpting, the Professor concocts a ghastly scheme
involving murder and revenge.

Always a little too into his work to begin with, the
now demented Professor turns to murder and body
snatching to provide the materials for his wax display.
To complicate the gruesome plotline, a beautiful damsel
enters the story and stumbles onto the Professor's
fiendish secret. The corpses continue to pile up until the
climatic ending in which the Professor's ghoulish deeds
are rewarded with a tumble into a boiling vat of wax,
while the damsel is saved at the last possible moment
by her dashing love interest.

Not only were audiences and critics alike thrilled with
the film and its high creep factor, but *House of Wax* was
also one of the first movies to hit the big screen in 3-D,
helping to usher in the 3-D craze that swept the industry
in the early 1950s. After all, the film did have everything

The Palace of Wax.

movie goers needed to scare them silly with large doses of murder, mystery, raging fires, a deformed killer, and a dark museum full of ominous wax figures.

Of course, most of us don't really believe that such dark tales exist outside of the big screen, or then again, do they? On the edge of Grand Prairie, just west of Dallas, is a modern curiosity known as the Palace of Wax, where once inside, the truth becomes stranger than fiction and as rumor has it, tragic spirits rise to haunt dark and twisted passageways.

Located on Palace Parkway, Louis Tussaud's Palace of Wax & Ripley's *Believe It or Not* Museum sits like a Sultan's palace straight from the pages of Richard Burton's, *The Arabian Nights*. Fashioned after King George IV's royal pavilion at Brighton, its façade runs a dizzying gamut of Indo Gothic architecture, complete with a central onion-shaped dome, overhanging eves, minarets, and flying pennants. Stepping inside the 41,000 square-foot building is like walking into a colorful dream where wax figures crafted after famous personalities await, ranging from characters of the old west to classic movie monsters.

In addition to the waxworks, is a bizarre collection of oddities gathered by famed Robert Ripley as he traveled the world in search of the strange and down right unbelievable. Included in the rather macabre collection are items such as a 4,000-year-old mummy's coffin, a mask made of human flesh, shrunken heads, and P. T. Barnum's "Fiji" mermaid.

As if all of that wasn't enough to overload the average visitor's weird button, then a confusing trip through the museum's elaborate maze of mirrors will.

The Palace of Wax, which originated as the Southwest Historical Wax Museum, opened its doors to the public in September of 1963, at the Texas State Fair Grounds in Dallas. Created by William Bolton and his associates, John Prather and J. C. Brown, the attraction displayed scenes of western gun fights as well as historical figures from Texas's past, such as Cynthia Ann Parker and Antonio Lopez

Santa Anna. Other personalities to be featured in the line up included the likes of the infamous Bonnie and Clyde, President John F. Kennedy, and the King himself, Elvis Presley. Included in the price of admission, the museum also boasted not only the 1934, Ford V8 in which bank robbers Bonnie and Clyde were gunned down in, but also the largest collection of firearms once owned by famous outlaws and heroes of the old west.

So popular was the wax museum that families came from all over the southwest to gawk at the life-like displays of history captured in wax. Crowds continued to pour through the museum until a decision was made to move the exhibit to Grand Prairie in 1972. Renamed the Wax Museum of the Southwest and under new ownership, the museum grew bigger and better than before, billing itself as the largest wax museum in all the southwest.

An Unusual Twist

It wasn't until 1984, that our story begins to take an unusual twist when a twenty-three year old museum employee named Lori Ann Wilson began complaining of abdominal pains. After a visit to the hospital, she was admitted for an appendectomy, but immediately into the procedure, the surgeon noted that her appendix was healthy and so aborted the operation.

Perplexed by her symptoms, the hospital elected to keep her for further testing, but over the course of just a few days, her condition deteriorated and she died from unknown causes. Grand Prairie police detectives at the time were skeptical about her death and began to suspect that perhaps Lori Ann Wilson had been poisoned. With nothing to go on other than the sneaky suspicion that something sinister was occurring, the police could do little more than wait for the murderer to slip up and show his hand.

Three years later, they would get their chance as the poisoner struck again, claiming the life of the museum's co owner, Patricia "Patsy" Wright, who was found dead in her Arlington apartment. This time there was no mistaking the cause of death. An autopsy revealed that Patsy had indigested cough syrup laced with strychnine poison, which consequently also causes severe abdominal pain prior to death. Closing in, the police now had two murder victims connected to the wax museum. Then suddenly, a third crime was committed that brought a new suspect to light who promised to hold the key to it all.

Late one night in October of 1988, a fire broke out in the wax museum, which raged through the structure destroying much of the building and all of the precious wax figures. The main suspect in the arson case was a man name Stanley Poynor, who police began to think might be involved in the previous museum murders as well.

Poynor was arrested for the fire and a careful search of his home revealed clues that reinforced the belief that Poynor was their man, including news clipping of the murders, photographs of the museum, and several airline tickets to various locations. Nonetheless, the police were forced to let him go based on a lack of evidence. But if Grand Prairie detectives thought they had heard the last of Stanley Poynor, they were wrong.

A Piece of the Puzzle

In September of 1998, Poynor was again in trouble, this time for breaking into an undamaged portion of the ruined museum in an attempt to steal financial ledgers, and once again, he managed to escape justice by posting a small bond. This time however, the man who had avoided the clutches of the law so many times before would find that his luck was running out.

A short time after his release, Poynor was shot to death by a Dallas police officer working traffic control in Oak Lawn. He died at the scene of the incident from gun shot wounds to the head, torso, and upper extremities.

The details are sketchy at best, but it seems that he struck a police officer with his car who was stopping traffic at the intersection of Rawlings and Throckmorton Streets. The officer, who was flipped onto the hood of Poynor's car, began firing through the windshield when Poynor purposefully began swerving to throw him off and refused to stop.

In the end, little is known about Stanley Poynor's life or just what his connection to the wax museum truly was. He was known to have a long criminal history including prior arrests for arson, but with his death, any remaining leads in the museum murder case simply dried up.

Up From the Ashes

In January of 1990, the former owners of the Wax Museum of the Southwest announced plans to rebuild the museum from the charred ruins of the old, and so after a flurry of construction, the Palace of Wax rose in its place. A few new walls and a fresh coat of paint however, wouldn't be enough to dispel the tragedies of the past and misfortunes continued to follow.

In August of 2007, police responded to a call from the museum's night manager who had startled three would-be thieves attempting to rob the company safe. One of the burglars was apprehended immediately, while the remaining two fled on foot to a nearby hotel. Following a brief shootout, one of the men surrendered to authorities and another was killed.

Two months later, the museum again found itself in jeopardy when a malfunctioning ceiling fan caught fire. Luckily, the new sprinkler system extinguished the blaze before it had the chance to spread to other parts of the building. Although there was some water damage, none of the costly wax displays were destroyed.

Fires, murders, police shootouts; if that wasn't enough to inspire a few ghost stories, then nothing would, and since the reopening of the museum almost seventeen years ago, the place has been rife with them. Even though no one would come forward and officially verify the chilling accounts you are about to hear, I did manage to run into a few employees in the parking lot who were willing to give me the "unofficial" version.

The "Unofficial" Version

Since working at the museum, some of the employees have encountered the strong smell of burning wood in certain areas of the building, throwing the staff into a panic on more than one occasion. Even though no source for the smell can be found, workers find it odd that in these instances the room often becomes bone chillingly cold. At other times, usually when alone, workers will hear the muffled whisper of conversation punctuated by the sound of a painful whimper.

Those who are forced to move about the museum performing tasks by themselves, often feel like they are being watched. Granted, the realistic displays can be unnerving enough, especially in the Hollywood movie monster section, but those who have experienced the feeling for themselves claim that it's something more than that.

Even the building's internal security system seems to be affected at times, and on numerous occasions the motion detectors placed throughout will trigger, even though the place it empty.

One last story I just couldn't pass up was told to me by another anonymous employee with all of the genuine sincerity and nervousness he could muster. Late one night while making his rounds through a dark hallway lit only by the subdued glare of shaded lamps, he suddenly began to feel as if he was not alone. A burning smell filled the hallway, and as he looked back behind him, he noticed something disturbing.

One of the many creepy characters that inhabit the Palace of Wax.

The floor, which was covered in a thick layer of ground fog produced by machines as part the particular display, began to suddenly part, as if something were moving toward them. Not waiting to find out what it was, the employee tore through the remaining exhibits, not stopping until he reached the safety of the well-lit ticket counter. From that day, the employee claims he will not enter some portions of the museum alone.

Reflections...

Despite the carnival like atmosphere that pervades the place, the museum's past reads like something straight from a horror movie script. No one knows for sure who or what haunts the building, but given its tragic history there are certainly a lot of candidates. Regardless of the attempts by museum officials to gloss over the incidents of the past, the truth usually has a way of coming to the surface anyway.

Perhaps that might even be our answer. Maybe something doesn't want us to forget what happened there.

The wax museum after all is a wonderful place and I always love to visit it, but it is easy to see how some of the spookier exhibits could give birth to tales of haunting specters. Those who have run into the spirits of the museum are convincingly adamant about their experiences and nothing will sway them otherwise. To this day, the wax museum continues to hold its secrets deep inside, waiting for someone to explore its corridors and perhaps solve its mysteries.

The Louis Tussaud's Palace of Wax and
Ripley's "Believe It or Not" Museum
601 Palace Parkway
Grand Prairie, Texas 75050
Phone: 972.263.2391
Web: www.palaceofwax.com

The Legend of Ghost Mountain

The gates to the Pleasant Valley Cemetery.

Now it is the time of night
That the graves, all gaping wide,
Every one lets forth his sprite
In the church-way paths to glide

—William Shakespeare,
"A Midsummer Night's Dream"

Pleasant Valley Cemetery

Among the rolling hills that lay between the lapping shores of Joe Pool Lake and the historic town of Cedar Hill, sits the Pleasant Valley Cemetery, a place filled with as many ghostly legends as there are tombstones. As an ever-popular hangout for area teens looking to see who can scare one another the worst, Pleasant Valley is known by a host of sinister names, including Witch Mountain and Old Spook Hill. However, for as long as spooky tales have been told about the place (and that's a long time) most have referred to it colorfully as Ghost Mountain.

Planted atop a rise with forests of dense cedar marching up its northern and eastern slopes, the wedge-shaped burial ground is surrounded with dense thickets of thorn and prickly cactus. Further complicating matters is the unceasing amount of new residential construction in the area and the changing street names, both of which have effectively hidden the cemetery from all, but a few of the locals familiar with the area.

The nearby township of Cedar Hill was founded around the 1850s, along a branch of the old Chisholm Trail as it meandered its way to Fort Worth. Many of those who settled the area were lured here by land grants from the Peters Colony, which promised rolling hills among lush prairie fields and vast holdings of cedar forests. Some came from as far as Kansas and Illinois, traveling up to six weeks by river and wagon to find a new home.

When they arrived, however, they quickly learned that the prairie wasn't as Eden-like as the brochures claimed it would be. In fact, they say the prairie grass grew as tall as a man's head while sitting on horseback and that teams of Texas Rangers were recruited to pull logs behind their horses to flatten the grass and provide passage.

Yet still they came, and in no time flat, a tiny hamlet of cedar logged cabins sprang up among the hills. In 1856, the town experienced its first real setback when a fierce tornado swept through the area destroying all of the cabins as if they were simple matchsticks and claiming the lives of as many as nine people. Yet, true to the pioneering spirit that marked those first Texans, the townsfolk of Cedar Hill began picking up their lives and one by one the cabins rose again.

From that time on the town grew and with the coming of the railroad in 1882, the settlement received a much needed economic boost. By 1915, the community was strongly established with three churches, two banks, and numerous other businesses, and today it is considered one of Dallas County's oldest settlements.

Jacob Gardner Boydstun and his family were the first to settle the land on which the cemetery now stands in 1848. As a deeply religious man, Jacob donated three acres of his land for the building of a church on the northeast corner of the claim. Although the small country church that grew there would not survive the ravages of time, the cemetery that sprang up next to it did, with Jacob Boydstun and his wife, Drusilla, becoming its first occupants. As time went on and the countryside around it changed considerably, the cemetery fell prey to the damaging effects of both the elements and vandals. Weeds choked its quiet paths, and portions of its northern section containing early African-American graves, were eroding into a neighboring creek bed.

Grave Robbing and Other Dark Desecrations

Far more destructive than anything nature could throw at it however, was the damaging effects people had on the ancient burial grounds. In the 1990s, Ghost Mountain witnessed a rash of vandalism as housing developments started to spring up in sight of the cemetery. Headstones were unceremoniously overturned or broken while trash and discarded beer cans littered the ground.

But far worse than any of these were the incidents of grave robbing and desecration. News articles from the time recount that bodies were being exhumed during the dead of night by grisly body snatchers. Caskets were being torn open and either all or parts of the bodies were being removed.

Although the culprits were never apprehended, nor the missing bodies recovered, local residents finally decided that they'd had enough. Now, thanks to the efforts of frequent police patrols and local citizen's groups much of the damage has been repaired, and those interned there can sleep again peacefully. On May 20, 1995, the Texas Historical Commission named the site a Texas historical landmark.

Perhaps it's the isolated nature of the cemetery itself or maybe the fact that body snatchers once plied their morbid trade here, but Ghost Mountain is thought by those who know its stories to be a place that is haunted.

The Deadly Curse and the Prowling Goatman

Most of the accounts are legends really—stories told by teenagers on a Saturday night, daring to see whose brave enough to enter the cemetery's gates after dark. For instance, one legend that has endured through the years, claims that Ghost Mountain is the meeting site of a secret coven of devil worshipers, who gather under the full moon each month to practice their dark arts. Any poor soul unlucky enough to chance upon one of these dark gatherings, runs the risk of having a curse rain down upon their head.

It's even said that a group of seven teenagers decided to test the truth of the claim once by entering the cemetery under a full moon. Slinking through the headstones, they came upon a blazing fire surrounded by black-robed figures chanting in an arcane language.

Unfortunately, one teen crept too close to the light of the fire and was discovered. With a shout, the teens sprang up and raced for their car—hotly pursued by the dark cultists. Jumping into the vehicle they sped off into the night with only the thought of putting as many miles between them and the cemetery as possible.

Yet if they thought they had escaped the danger unscathed they would be wrong.

As the teen's vehicle tore away from the cemetery in panic, one of the cultists hurled a curse after them. While driving home that night, their vehicle collided with another car, killing four of the teens inside. Now they say the spirits of those four teenagers walk the grounds of Ghost Mountain each night, cursed to haunt the cemetery for eternity.

If that tale isn't enough to keep the curious away, then perhaps another legend associated with the place involving a character common in many Texas tales known as the goatman will. No one really knows from where the beast sprang—only that he has been spotted under rickety bridges, moonlit lakes, and ancient cemeteries throughout the state.

Descriptions of the horrid creature vary from story to story, but by most accounts, the goatman isn't something you'd want to run into at a cemetery late at night. Half man and half goat, with curving fangs and sharp claws, the disfigured monster is said to prowl the environs of Ghost Mountain feeding off the corpses of the dead. Oh yeah, and anything else that happens to run across its path as well.

Grave Warnings

There are many tales such as these just waiting for someone to listen to them. Of course, each differs slightly with the telling, but all carry with them the warning that Ghost Mountain is no place to be caught after the sun has set over the hills and the spirits come out to roam.

With these stories also come the ghost hunters, who have for years investigated its corpse-filled slopes with mixed results. Many believe that the true source of the haunting is not the result of devil-worshiping

The graves of Ghost Mountain.

cultists or monsters in the night, but of vandalism. Often, those cemeteries that have had the high levels of paranormal activity have also had the greatest amount of vandalism.

The belief that desecrating the body or the grave causes the spirit of the corpse to rise in anger dates back to the time of the Egyptians, and the great lengths they went to protect the bodies of their dead from tomb robbers. Even during the height of Greece and Rome, from which we still derive many of our customs and laws, there were prohibitions against improper burials. Desecrating a body or tomb carried with it stiff fines and punishments. Even passing by an unburied body and not offering some token of burial could land one in deep trouble with the law. After all, no one wanted an angry ghost running around causing problems.

Who knows what truly walks the dark paths of Ghost Mountain. All we do know is that the stories all tell us to stay away. A word of caution for those planning a little "nocturnal visit" of their own; the gates close at 7 pm and visiting after hours is highly discouraged by local law enforcement. Then again, there might be worse things to fear on Ghost Mountain after dark.

Pleasant Valley Cemetery
located off Texas Plume Road,
southwest of Cedar Hill.

Interview with a Big D Ghost Hunter

Barry Turnage

The history of ghost hunting is replete with colorful characters that devoted their lives and talents to unraveling the mysteries of the paranormal. From the spiritualists, churchmen, and scientists that graced its stage in the early years, to the celebrity ghost hunters of today, there is an indelible debt owed the men and women who have given so much to the field.

One of those individuals is Barry Turnage—a veteran ghost hunter who has worked tirelessly to investigate claims of the paranormal, as well as educate the public with his knowledge of ghosts. From the wind-swept ghost towns of Texas's past to the dark burial grounds of its cities' cemeteries, it could easily be said that Barry Turnage is a man who knows his ghosts.

The following is an account of some of his fascinating experiences and a brief glimpse into what it takes to be a Big D ghost hunter.

Q: Barry, how did you first become interested in ghosts?

A: Well, in the mid 1970s, I was in the Coast Guard, stationed at Governor's Island, New York. Late one night I had the mid watch, which required me to patrol one of the large buildings there on base. All of the buildings (barracks, classrooms, etc.) were connected at their center by an attic with a fire door. Some of these buildings had stood since the Revolutionary War, so they were very old and had a lot of history. I would make my rounds through the attic and punch a clock. It was a fire watch really. There were a lot of scary stories about that attic, so when I went through it, I tried to get out of there as fast as I could. It was one large room with a single bulb hanging from the ceiling, filled with desks, boxes, and old school lockers.

On one of my rounds, I kept hearing noises and thought my mind was playing tricks on me. About half way through the attic, a set of metal lockers against the wall began banging, one right after the other, bam, bam, bam! I ran out of there and didn't even punch the clock that night.

Come to find out, I wasn't the only one to have these experiences, but no one wanted to talk about them. That's when I began to take an interest in the paranormal.

Q: How did you get involved in ghost hunting?

A: I was originally involved with another group studying UFOs called M.U.F.O.N. I had gotten out of it for several years when a friend of mine from the group called me up and asked if I wanted to go on a ghost tour of the Fort Worth Stockyards. My wife and I went and thought it was great. Later, another researcher whom I met on the tour named Carl Hullett called me and asked if I wanted to be part of a new ghost hunting group he was putting together.

Q: Can you tell me a little bit about the ghost hunting movement?

A: When I first got involved in ghost hunting, it still hadn't caught on like it has today. It seems like over the last few years, it's suddenly become very popular. That's good in the sense that people are learning more about it, after all, we want to educate people about the paranormal. However, I find it troubling that people getting into ghost hunting haven't received enough of the true basics needed to really experience the paranormal the way it should be...and we're here to help with that.

Q: What types of people are normally drawn to hunting ghosts?

A: Well, it helps to be a free thinker, someone willing to examine the evidence and make a decision based on sound reasoning. Most of the ghost hunters I know are very intelligent people.

Q: After all these years of investigations, what do you think ghosts really are?

A: I definitely believe in them and I've seen and heard enough during my investigations, that it's hard not to. Actually, no one has ever proven to me that there aren't ghosts. Has there been any breakthrough proving they do exist? No, but there are enough little tidbits piling up to make me believe. Are they the souls of people who won't move on? To be honest, I don't know. That's what I'm trying to find out. That's the million dollar question.

Q: When you go out on ghost hunts, what type of equipment do you like to use?

A: The list of what I've found useful over the years is endless, but some of the standard equipment you'll find in any ghost hunter's bag includes tape recorders, both digital and the old shoebox type, as well as a good digital camera. Before that, I was using a 35 mm camera, but you end up wasting a lot of film with those. Flashlights are a must and a few glow sticks in case the batteries run out. Our group uses EMF meters a lot, but unfortunately, they're too expensive for most. I also use a thermal scanner to check for temperature changes in the environment. I have a bag full of stuff that I have yet to use, but you never know when it will come in handy. Recently, I've had to lighten the bag up some because it's gotten so heavy it's, starting to hurt my back.

Q: One of the areas you're best known for is your work on EVPs; could you tell us a little about that?

A: EVP stands for electronic voice phenomena and is the process of capturing spirit voices that normally couldn't be heard with the human ear. It's at a different decibel than what the human ear registers. It can however, be heard through tape recorders, television sets, and radios to name a few. Normally when we think we have an EVP, we run it through software programs designed to look for such anomalies and filter out the background noise so they can be heard better.

Q: What's the strangest EVP you have ever collected during an investigation?

A: I would have to say it was at Miss Molly's B & B in Fort Worth, Texas. It used to be an old bordello and the owner agreed to let us come in and conduct an investigation. We set up our audio equipment and then left for dinner. While we were gone we left the recorders going for about forty-five minutes. Months later, I went back and listened to the tapes from that night. What I heard was about forty-five minutes of tape squashed into about two minutes, with weird growling sounds throughout. That one's a little freaky.

Q: What do you think is the best piece of evidence you've come across to support a belief in ghosts?

A: I've had some experiences that although doesn't prove ghosts exist, certainly adds to the mountain of evidence in favor of them. I once had something grab hold of my ponytail during an investigation and pull my head back into the wall. I was alone at the time, so I cannot prove to anyone else that it happened, but I know it did. There are other things I've encountered like spirit rapping or knocking and even disembodied voices, which point in the direction of ghosts. As far as one single piece of evidence that proves the existence of ghosts, well I haven't seen that yet. I don't think anyone has.

Q: What is the scariest moment you have had while ghost hunting?

A: I've had my hair stand on end more than once, but the worst was while I was working security at the Baker Hotel during public tours of the place. What happened was, someone had split off from one of the tour groups and Carl Hullett and I went to search for them. We were walking down the hallway looking into rooms with our flashlights when we stopped near the elevator shaft. Carl wanted to look inside, so I held the flashlight for him while he pried the doors open. Out of the corner of my eye, I saw something move at the end of the hallway. I whipped around out of instinct and Carl yelled out "where's my light," and that's when my hair got pulled. My head went straight into the wall behind me. Man, my hair stood straight up on the back of my neck. It took me a couple of minutes after that to compose myself. That was the first time I was ever touched by a spirit.

Q: Can you tell us about some of the dangers associated with ghost hunting?

A: First of all, never go by yourself. You always need to have someone with you for a number of reasons. Someone needs to be there to validate what you see and hear. Two witnesses are better than one. The second is in case you get hurt or in trouble of some kind. Plus, you don't get so freaked out in a scary cemetery if there's someone with you.

Whenever you enter a building or property, you always need to ask permission. Not doing so would make your evening a real bummer if you got yourself arrested for trespassing.

You also need to be careful because a lot of these old buildings could cave right in on you.

Finally, the living can be far worse than the dead and you might run into someone who doesn't want you there. Besides having fun, you need to make sure you're safe first.

Q: We hear a lot about ghosts in the media with television shows on ghost hunting and haunted places; what impact do you think that has played on the field?

A: A lot. I really do. I know that by talking to many ghost hunters, they tell me they were first introduced to it through shows like *Ghost Hunters*. Even my pizza delivery boy talks to me about the show when he comes to my door.

Q: What kind of advice would you give to someone wanting to get involved in ghost hunting?

A: Research, research, and more research. Read everything you can find on the subject; then take that only with a grain of salt. Most groups are real cautious about letting new people in, but they're not opposed to answering questions. Who knows, once they get to know you better, they may just ask you to join. You don't just want to jump into this field and spend a bunch of money on expensive equipment without knowing what you're doing.

Suggested Readings

Many a harrowing text on the history and nature of ghosts has been written since the invention of the published word. In fact, one of the oldest books known to man is an ancient Sumerian text, later known as the *Gilgamesh*, which includes a story about heroes traveling to the underworld and ghosts rising from the ground. Since that distant time, man has been studying and writing about ghosts. Everything from horror stories to firsthand accounts by ghost hunters. Nowadays, you can even find books that list all the great places to eat and sleep that have a reputation for being haunted. In the hopes of broadening your ghostly horizons, I've included a list of books that may aid you on your journey. This is by no means a complete list, but think of it rather as an introduction into a haunted world of mystery, suspense, and excitement.

In General:

Apparitions
> by G. N. M. Tyrrell

Apparitions and Ghosts
> by Andrew MacKenzie

Apparitions and Survival of Death
> by Raymond Bayless

The Case for Ghosts: An Objective Look at the Paranormal
> by J. Allen Danelek

Complete Book of Ghosts and Poltergeists
> by Leonard R. Ashley

Complete Idiot's Guide to Ghosts and Hauntings
    by Tom Ogden

Encyclopedia of Ghosts and Spirits
    by Rosemary Ellen Guiley

Ghost: Investigating the Other Side
    by Katherine Ramsland

The Ghost Hunter's Guidebook
    by Troy Taylor

Ghost Hunting: How to Investigate the Paranormal
    by Loyd Auerbach

Ghost Hunting: True Stories of Unexplained Phenomena from The Atlantic Paranormal Society
    by Jason Hawes, Grant Wilson, and Michael Jan
        Friedman

Houses of Horror
    by Hans Holzer

How to be a Ghost Hunter: Field Guide for the Paranormal Investigator
    by Richard Southall, R. H. Southall,
    and Michael Ed. Hill (Editor)

How to Hunt Ghosts: a Practical Guide
    by Joshua P. Warren

True Hauntings: Spirits with a Special Purpose
    by Hazel Denning

The World's Most Haunted Place: From the Secret Files of Ghostvillage.com
    by Jeff Belanger

On North Texas:

Best Tales of Texas Ghosts
  by Docia Schultz Williams

Ghosts in the Graveyard: Texas Cemetery Tales
  by Olyve Hallmark Abbott

Ghosts of North Texas
  by Mitchel Whitington

Ghost Stories of Old Texas, Vol. 1
  by Zinita Fowler

Ghost Stories of Texas
  by Jo-Anne Christensen

Ghost Stories of Texas
  by Ed Seyers

Haunted Texas: A Travel Guide
  by Scott Williams

Phantoms of the Plains
  by Docia Schultz Williams

Spirits of Texas
  by Vallie Fletcher Taylor

A Texas Guide to Haunted Restaurants, Taverns and Inns
  by Robert & Anne Wlodarski

Texas Haunted Forts
  by Elaine Coleman

Ghost Groups of the Big D

Over the years, a grassroots movement of ghost hunters has cropped up across the country made up of individuals from just about every walk of life. These men and women dedicate themselves to exploring the mysteries of the unknown and seeking out proof that something exists beyond the materiel world we inhabit. Dallas and the surrounding area is no exception to this and contains a number of ghost hunting groups ready to dash out on a case at a moment's notice. Each brings with them a unique perspective to the field of ghost hunting and various investigative techniques that range from the use of mediums to high-tech equipment.

The following is a list of ghost hunting groups active in the area and open to investigation requests. Not only do most of these groups work for free, but they also publish web sites filled with a vast amount of information. With just a click of the mouse, you can find everything from pictures of apparitions to discussions on the latest ghost hunting tools. If all else fails and you cannot secure the assistance of one of these groups, then by all means, why not start your own.

Association for the Study of Unexplained Phenomenon
www.asup-texas.com

Carrollton Paranormal Society
www.carrolltonparanormalsociety.com

Dagulf's Ghost
www.dagulfsghost.com

DFW Ghost Hunters
www.dfwghosthunters.com

DFW Paranormal Research of North Texas
www.dfwparanormalresearch.com

Metroplex Paranormal Investigations
www.metroplexparanormalinvestigations.com

Paranormal Investigations of North Texas
www.hauntedtexasonline.com

The Phantom Hunters
www.thephantomhunters.com

Tarrant County Investigations of the Paranormal
www.tarrantcountyparanormal.com

Texas Paranormal Research Team
www.tprt.org

Shadow Lands
www.shadowlands.net

Although not a ghost hunting group, this web site provides an excellent index of haunted locations in both Texas and the continental United States.

White Noise Investigations
www.whitenoiseinvestigations.com

Spooky Tours

DFW Ghost Hunters provides guided tours of some of the spookiest locales in the Dallas area. Admission for most tours is nominal, and in addition to learning the history and legends of the sites, these ghost hunters show you how to use the latest ghost hunting equipment while guiding you through your very own investigation. Booking information can be found on their web site at **www.dfwghosthunters.com**.

More Boo for the Buck

Each year across America a sinister change takes place, from big cities to small towns, during the month of October. What were once ordinary homes, businesses, and fairgrounds are rapidly transformed into places of pure terror. Fake cobwebs complete with rubber spiders fill windows, as Styrofoam headstones pop up, and prerecorded Halloween sound effects fill the air. Unbelievably, long lines of costume-clad children form outside. Each would-be victim waiting for the chance to scream their way through places with names such as Doctor Demento's Dungeon of Doom or the always popular Haunted Mansion of Blood.

The history of haunted attractions in the U.S. is thought to have evolved in the early 1900s, as traveling sideshows sought to capitalize on the ghostly interest of the spiritualist movement sweeping the country. Since that time, commercial haunted houses have come a long way, incorporating the latest technology in animatronics, theatrical sets, lighting, and other special effects.

According to current industry estimates, there are over 3,000 haunted attractions operating in North America alone during the month of October. This translates into big business, with about 300 to 500 million dollars in ticket sales each year—and growing. That, in turn, goes to support an entire trade of vendors, costumes makers, building material suppliers, and advertisers. In addition, over eighty percent of these attractions are either operated by charitable organizations or they donate a portion of their proceeds to worthwhile groups such as the Boys and Girl's Club or the Special Olympics.

So if your looking for a *spooktacular* time, and your not one of the faint of heart, you might try one of the following attractions located in and around Dallas. I warn you, however, none of these haunted house guaranties that once you enter, you'll ever be heard from again… Some even suggests you wear your toe tag on the way in.

The Boneyard Haunted House
3000 E. Pioneer Parkway
Arlington, Texas 76010

Over fifty chilling scenes of the macabre seamlessly blended together for a truly frightening experience. This dark attraction has been submitted to *the Guinness Book of World Records* as the largest walkthrough haunted house in the world. Proceeds from the attraction go to benefit the local Special Olympics. For more information, visit their website at **www.boneyard.org.**

Chaos Haunted House
800 W. Kennedale Parkway
Kennedale, Texas 76060

Includes not one, but three haunted houses, as well as a hayride spooky enough for all ages. Proceeds go to benefit Special Needs People, Inc. For more information, visit their website at **www.chaoshauntedhouse.com**.

Dallas Sacregrounds
2001 Irving Boulevard
Dallas, Texas 75207

Three truly terrifying attractions including the Necrotorium, a zombie infested cemetery, the Terrortorium, a grisly maze of fright, and the Hallucinatorium, a 3-D realm of insanity. For more information, visit their website at **www.dallasscaregrounds.com**.

The Dungeon of Doom
201 W. Main Street
Arlington, Texas 76010

Descend into the dark and deadly basement of the Arlington Museum of Art, in what has been billed by the *Dallas Observer* as, "the best haunted house in the DFW metroplex." All of the proceeds go to the Museum of Art children's education programs. For more information, visit their website at **www.dungeonofdoomtexas.com.**

The Forest of Fear
Loyd Park at Joe Pool Lake
3401 Ragland Road
Grande Prairie, Texas 75052

A haunted campground on the shores of Joe Pool Lake complete with camp decorating contests, pumpkin carving, and a haunted hayride through a dark forest filled with ghouls and goblins. For more information, visit their website at **www.loydpark.com.**

Fright Fest at Six Flags Over Texas
2201 Road to Six Flags
Arlington, Texas 76010

Welcome to the land of ghosts and ghouls, haunted houses and amusement rides, live shows and just plain fun. This is a Halloween theme park like only Six Flags can pull off. Eat hot dogs with Dracula or scream your way through haunt-themed roller coasters. For more information, visit their website at **www.sixflags.com.**

Mead Manor House
6921 Bennet Lawson Road
Mansfield, Texas 76063

Advertised as being "built with a passion for scaring people, not just selling tickets," this haunted attraction comprises approximately 8,000 feet of dark twisting corridors and a staff of over fifty zombies and homicidal maniacs dripping with fresh blood. For more information, visit their website at **www.meadmanor.com**.

Nightmare at the Wax Museum
601 Palace Parkway
Grande Prairie, Texas 75050

Walk through a collection of the world's most famous monsters including Dracula, Freddy Kruger, and the Wolfman, but beware, some of these ghastly statues are real and hungry for blood. For more information, visit their website at **www.palaceofwax.com.**

Nightmares Haunted House
5515 S. Cooper Street
Arlington, Texas 76017

Billed as more of a traditional haunted house, their website claims "an adrenaline filled, jaw dropping, heart pounding experience that will leave you breathless." For more information, visit their website at **www.nightmaresarlington.com.**

Phantom's Haunted House
1300 Robert B. Cullum Boulevard
Dallas, Texas 75210

After ten years of scaring Texans silly, these people really have it down. They even go as far as to claim that "those who actually made it through all the way were usually running out the door screaming, crying, and yelling." For more information, visit their website at **www.phantomshaunt.com.**

Reindeer Manor
410 Houston School Road
Red Oak, Texas 75154

This one has just about everything needed to scare the wits out of you, including psychics, a sword swallower, monster maze, horror movie theater, the 13th Street Morgue, and finally, Reindeer Manor itself. For more information, visit their website at **www.reindeermanor.com.**

Screams Halloween Theme Park
2511 FM 66
Waxahachie, Texas 75167

Considered the world's largest Halloween theme park with four haunted houses including the Castle of Darkness, Terrorvision 3-D, Arcane Asylum, and the Black Hole Experience. If you don't think that's enough fright, then add in the Maze of the Macabre, the Ghoulish Graveyard, Scaryoke, Mythical Monster Museum, games, rides, food, face painters, and fortune tellers. For more information, visit their website at **www.screamspark.com.**

The Slaughter House
2020 N. Lamar Street
Dallas, Texas 75202

Watch out for this creepy attraction. Their own disclaimer reads, "very graphic and not intended for small children or anyone with a weak stomach or heart." For more information visit their website at **www.weslaughter.com**.

Tayman Graveyard
Between Midlothian and Cedar Hill
Take Highway 67 south from Dallas,
exit Shiloh and turn right.
Follow the signs to the parking lot.

Brought to you by Boy Scout Troop 202 and includes the Tayman Haunted Funeral Home, Haunted Mine Shaft, and a spooky hayride. Don't be fooled by the thought of boy scouts, however, rather than wholesome do-gooders, think undead monsters welding chainsaws. For more information visit their website at **www.taymangraveyard.com**.

Thrillvania & Verdun Manor
2330 County Road 138
Terrell, Texas 75161

Six different haunted attractions, games, food, and entertainment. This deadly attraction includes Verdun Manor, Voodoo Bayou, Cassandra's Labyrinth of Terror, Dr. Lycan's Trail of Torment, and Granny Lupus's Séance Theatre. Selected *by Haunt World Magazine* as the 4th best haunted attraction in the country. For more information, visit their website at **www.thrillvania.com**.

Glossary

Included is a list of terms most commonly found in the field of the paranormal. Whether as an aspiring ghost hunter, a seasoned professional investigator, or simply someone who loves to read about the supernatural, the following definitions are essential to understanding the phenomena contained in this book. Although this is by no means a complete list, and you may also find slight variations depending on whom you talk to, it is a good start.

Anomaly

Comes from the Greek work *anomalia*, meaning something unnatural or unusual. Anomalies refer to anything strange appearing on film, sound recordings, or any other unexplained evidence gathered on an investigation.

Apparition

The unexpected appearance of a person, animal, or object in the form of a ghost, phantom, specter, or wraith. The word originated in the Middle English *apparicioun*, meaning to appear.

Earthbound

Describes a spirit or soul trapped on the material plane in the form of an apparition, ghost, phantom, specter, or wraith. This usually occurs near the place of their death or some other familiar location. The reasons for a spirit becoming earthbound are varied and complicated.

Ectoplasm

A phenomenon used to describe unusual mist or fog in photographs taken by researchers and is thought to be a sign of spirit activity. The term originally derived from the Greek words *ektos* and *plasma*, meaning "exteriorized substance."

EMF (electromagnetic field meter)

A device used to measure disturbances in the magnetic fields, which are often associated with spirit manifestations.

EVP (electronic voice phenomena)

Capturing spirit voices or ghostly sounds with audio recording devices or other electronic means.

Ghost

The soul or spirit of a dead person returned to haunt a location. The word originates from the Middle English term *gost*, meaning spirit or breath.

Haunting

To visit, appear, or inhabit in the form of an apparition or ghost. Hauntings are usually confined to a specific location and for an extended period of time that may include hundreds of years.

Hot spot

A location frequented by paranormal activity such as cold spots, orbs, ghosts, etc.

Ley lines

Thought to be invisible lines of natural energy running across the earth. Early humans were thought to have built sacred sites and burial grounds along their course. Some theorize that many haunted sites can be found where two such lines cross creating a nodule of super-charged energy that feeds the haunting.

Manifestation

The attempt by a spirit or ghost to materialize itself or influence objects in the material world. This can include cold spots, disembodied voices, apparitions, or the movement of objects.

Medium
A person with the ability or talent to communicate with the spirits of the dead. Also known as psychics or sensitives, the term initially meant, "one who stands in the middle ground."

Orb
A sphere or globe of energy created by a spirit that may appear on film or digital images, but remains unseen in most cases to the naked eye. Dust, pollen, water vapor, and insects are know to produce the same effects and are designated as environmental orbs.

Paranormal or supernatural
Events that are beyond what is considered a normal experience or which defy scientific explanation.

Phenomenon
An observable fact, occurrence, or circumstance.

Séance
Describes the attempt by a group of individuals to contact spirits of the dead. Normally, a séance is led by one or more mediums who help channel the spirits. The term comes from the Old French, *seoir*, meaning simply—to sit.

Soul or spirit
Both terms are used interchangeably in the text and describe the immaterial, life essence, or personality center of each individual.

Thermometer
Any device that measures temperature fluctuations in the environment which may indicate the presence of a spirit.

Urban myths

Moderns stories or legends passed on from person to person, often changing with each telling. Although the origins of most urban myths are obscure and contain little supporting evidence, many are found to have some grain of truth to them.

Bibliography

Abbott, Olyve Hallmark. *Ghosts in the Graveyard: Texas Cemetery Tales*. Plano: Republic of Texas Press, 2002.

Acheson, Sam Hanna. *Dallas Yesterday*, edited by Lee Milazzo. Dallas: Southern Methodist University Press, 1977.

Anders, John. "Things that go cha-cha-cha in the night." *Dallas Morning News*, March 6, 1998.

Barry Turnage (Paranormal Researcher) interviewed by author, August 18, 2007.

Brunvand, Jan Harold. *The Vanishing Hitchhiker: American Urban Legends and Their Meanings*. New York: W. W. Norton & Company, Inc., 1981.

Chris Mosley (Paranormal Researcher) interviewed by author, October 24, 2007.

Cuellar, Catherine. "When ghosts inhabit your business year-round, Halloween is no big Deal." *Dallas Morning News*, October 31, 1999.

"The Ghost of White Rock." Backwoods to Border. Ed by J. Frank Dobie. Austin: Texas Folk-Lore Society, 1943.

Lich, Glen E., *The German Texans*. San Antonio: University of Texas, 1981.

Payne, Darwin. *Dallas, an Illustrated History*. Woodland Hills, CA: Windsor Publications, 1982.

Rogers, John Williams. *The Lusty Texans of Dallas*. New York: Dutton, 1951.

Syers, Ed. *Ghost Stories of Texas*. Waco: Texas Press, 1981.
Whittington, Mitchel. *Ghosts of North Texas*. Plano: Republic of Texas Press, 2002.

Williams, Docia Schultz. *Best Tales of Texas Ghosts*. Plano: Republic of Texas Press, 1998.

Wlodarski, Robert & Anne. *Texas Guide to Haunted Restaurants, Taverns and Inns*. Plano: Republic of Texas Press, 2001.